The 12

James Collins

Beacon Street Press
500 Beacon Drive
Oklahoma City, OK 73127
1-800-652-1144
www.swrc.com

Printed in the United States of America

ISBN 1-933641-51-7

The 12

Ancient Messages of Hope for Today's Dark World

James Collins

Dedication

I dedicate this book to twelve men who at one time or another had a profound influence on my life. This book is dedicated to Fred Hambrick, Bryant Oglesby, Emmett Oglesby, Luke Senior, Haskell Citty, Victor Balabagan, Edward Alford, Carl Smith, Ray Swinford, Jack Mills, Noah Hutchings, and Larry Spargimino.

None of these twelve men were my biological father. However, each one was a father figure at some point in my life. Each planted seeds that grew me into the man I am today. Thank you all for having the courage to speak the truth.

Acknowledgements

Anytime you pick up a book and glance at the cover, you see the name of the author or authors who wrote it. That might lead you to believe it was something they created or dreamt up all by themselves. I can tell you, after writing several books, that is the furthest thing from the truth. Yes, the author may choose the words and the order in which they appear on the page, but the ideas and concepts that are shared on those pages are the result of many years of living, breathing, learning, and being shaped by the people and things around them throughout their lifetime. What has ended up in this book, to a large degree, would not have come to be without many people and experiences that have impacted and inspired me along the way.

I am grateful to the staff at Southwest Radio Church. Thanks to Dr. Kenneth Hill, Matthew Hill, Marvin McElvany, Danny Phillips, Tabitha Cook, Donna Smith, Edward Webber, Alan Joy, and Matthew McElvany. Thank you, MiMi Davis, for your optimism and exuberance. I apologize for misspelling your name in my previous book. Thanks to Veronica Joy for her help with the cover design.

My most sincere thanks to Christi Killian for her support, advice, and expertise in editing and formatting this book.

Special thanks to my friend, Chris Enders, for helping me to develop the title for this book.

I would like to thank Dr. Larry Spargimino for his decades of mentorship, friendship, and support.

I also want to thank the congregation of Franklin Baptist Church in Norman, Oklahoma. I first preached through the Minor Prophets at Franklin

Baptist back in 2004. Much of this book comes from that sermon series.

Thank you, to my children, for giving me the time and space to write.

To my wife, Amanda: I love you very much. Thank you for your encouragement.

I thank God for all of you.

—James Collins

Contents

Introduction

What's in a name? William Shakespeare, in *Romeo and Juliet,* asked the question, "What's in a name?" Well, according to the business website Inc.com, a name can make or break a product. For instance, Clairol launched a curling iron called "Mist Stick" in Germany, even though "mist" is German slang for manure. Coors translated its slogan, "Turn It Loose," into Spanish, where it is a term for having to constantly go to the bathroom. Mercedes-Benz entered the Chinese market under the brand name "Bensi," which means "rush to die." Kentucky Fried Chicken had to change their slogan "finger-lickin' good" when they entered the Chinese market because the slogan translated to "We will eat your fingers off." The "Jolly Green Giant" had to change his name when the company expanded to Arabic nations because his name in Arabic means "intimidating green monster." I served as a Chaplain in the U.S. Army for many years. The soldiers gave me the nickname "Chappy." My unit once trained with soldiers from Germany. The German soldier laughed when the troops called me "Chappy" because it is a brand of dog food in Germany.

The label we attach to a product can make a big difference in how it is received, and Augustine didn't do the twelve prophets any favors. Augustine, the Bishop of Hippo in North Africa who died in A.D. 430, was most likely the first to identify the Minor Prophets with the name "Minor Prophets"—which was an unfortunate choice of words. Neither their message nor ministry was minor in any way. In fact, there is one interesting fact that makes these twelve prophets significant: hundreds of years before Christ was born, the work of these twelve prophets was treated as one unit. As early as 200 B.C., these twelve works circulated as a single literary work. It was written on one scroll and recognized as a single book. The Jewish historian Josephus even numbered the books of the Old Testament in such a way that demonstrates that he thought of the twelve prophets as a single work. Taken as a single work, their total length matched that of Isaiah, Jeremiah, or Ezekiel.

Since the word "minor" designating a prophetic book does not appear in the Bible, many scholars argue that we should avoid it altogether. In fact, most Hebrew scholars even refer to them as "The Book of the Twelve" instead of as the Minor Prophets.

Major Prophet vs. Minor Prophet

What's the difference between a Major Prophet and a Minor Prophet? Well, there are four Major Prophets—Isaiah, Jeremiah, Ezekiel, and Daniel. The Major Prophets are called major because their prophecies were longer. The Minor Prophets are called minor because their prophecies were shorter. It has been my experience over the years when it comes to a preacher, people prefer a minor preacher over a major preacher. You could call the Major Prophets long-winded preachers. The Minor Prophets would have made modern church folks happy because they were short-winded preachers. However, little is much when God is in it. There are major messages contained in the writings of the Minor Prophets.

Unfortunately, in America today, the messages of the Minor Prophets are almost totally ignored. The Christian website Crossway recently released an infographic article about the Bible-reading habits of Americans. They surveyed six thousand people to learn how often they read the Bible and what portions of Scripture they tend to gravitate toward the most. They asked questions like, "Which section of the Bible do you read most often?" and "Which section do you find hardest to understand?" According to their research, most Bible readers read from the New Testament over fifty percent of the time. When Americans do read from the Old Testament, they most often read from Psalms, Proverbs, and the book of Genesis. At the bottom of the "most read list" were those pesky little Minor Prophets—specifically Obadiah and Nahum.

The Crossway article also makes it very clear as to why Americans spend so little time reading the prophets in general, and the Minor Prophets specifically: they are universally recognized as the most difficult books of the Bible to understand. About forty-five percent of Bible readers identified the Old Testament prophets as the most difficult to understand of all the Scriptures. So, I have made it my mission to rescue the Minor Prophets from the bottom of the Bible reading pool.

What Is a Prophet?

Did you know that on May 21, 2011, the world came to an end? Sort of. Well, not really at all. Despite thirteen predictions of the Rapture occurring and the world coming to an end by self-identified prophet Harold Camping, the world is still here. But right up until his last prophetic prediction, donors were supporting him to the tune of millions of dollars. Was Camping a prophet, a false prophet, or none of the above? What exactly is a prophet?

A biblical prophet was a man called by God to communicate the word of the Lord. He did not choose to be a prophet. Many God-called prophets didn't really want the job. Jonah comes to mind. A king may assume his authority because of his family lineage; a priest may be appointed or elected to his office; but a prophet was called by God to be His spokesman. Therefore, the messages of the Twelve should be understood as coming directly from God Himself.

When most people think of prophets, they tend to think about someone who foretold the future. However, the biblical prophets were not primarily foretellers of the future. Yes, they did speak of future events, but that was not their primary role.

The Prophets Spoke of Repentance

The prophets in the Bible had a fourfold ministry. First, they had the ministry of repentance. Biblical repentance means much more than just feeling sorry for your sins. It means more even than saying you're sorry for them. Biblical repentance means turning away from your sins and turning to embrace God. It means change—changing your mind about the way you've been living, changing your heart about the things you've been wrongly valuing, changing your actions and intentions into ones that are pleasing to God. The word "repent" means "to turn around." It literally means, "to change direction." It means, "I have turned around and I am walking a different way."

Repentance was the great mission of every prophet: not to frighten people with a message of inescapable doom, but to invite people to turn to the Lord. Even when they talked about the terrible things that would happen to those who persisted in evil, God's spokesmen had another purpose. It was to invite the lost to accept His salvation.

The Prophets Spoke of Revival

Second, the prophets had a ministry of revival. They would call the people to repent of their sin and return to God. Revival is an experience among God's people. It is for saved people. If you are lost, you have never been "vived." Only the "vived" can be revived. The prophets called for revival. They called for a spiritual awakening among God's people.

The Prophets Spoke of Revelation

Third, the prophets had a ministry of revelation. The Apostle Peter wrote that these great prophets were moved or borne along by the Holy Spirit. That is how God spoke through them. They forthtold the word and they foretold the future. The words of the prophets were written down, and they are the very words of God speaking to man.

The Prophets Spoke of Redirection

The prophets also had a ministry of redirection. During difficult times; during times of heartache and challenge; during times of adversity; during times of despair; during times when there was no good news and no hope, the prophets would direct the people's attention away from their problems. The prophets would direct the people's attention away from their problems and back to God, which would give them hope.

In my travels in ministry, I have walked in the footsteps of the Twelve. I walked where they walked both literally and spiritually. For example, like Jonah, I preached in Nineveh. During a military deployment to Iraq, I preached to a group of soldiers in the ruins of Nineveh. Also, like Jonah, there have been times in my life that I ran from God. So, I feel a connection with the Twelve.

The men who wrote the Book of the Twelve were my kind of preachers. They were old-fashioned, Holy Ghost, leather-lunged, pound on the pulpit preachers. They preached God's Word and they didn't care who they offended. They remind me of old-time evangelists, but they have some of the most relevant and contemporary messages that you will find anywhere in the Bible. Our modern world needs to hear the messages of these men. They could stand in any pulpit, they could stand before any crowd in America today, and their message would be up to date. Their message would be life-transforming. Their message would be the voice of God speaking to us today. That is something we need more of in this politically correct day and age.

This book was not meant to be a full commentary. It is intended to be incomplete. I hope this book leads you to a deeper Bible study. My prayer is that you will grasp the urgency and importance of the messages of the Twelve, and spend time learning about them from God's Word.

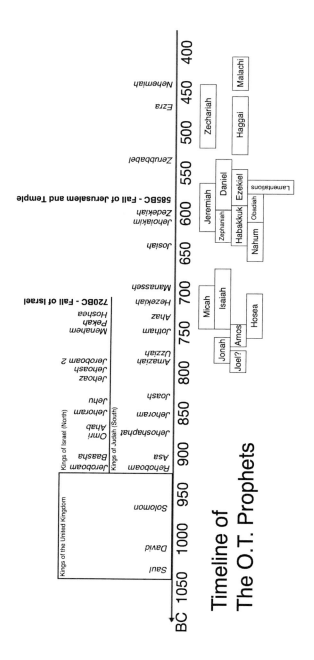

Timeline of
The O.T. Prophets

CHAPTER 1

God Loves the Unlovely

The beginning of the word of the Lord by Hosea. And the Lord said to Hosea, Go, take unto thee a wife of whoredoms and children of whoredoms: for the land hath committed great whoredom, departing from the Lord.

—Hosea 1:2

I remember watching Barbara Smith care for her husband, Carl, in his final months. A year or so earlier, my friend Carl was diagnosed with amyotrophic lateral sclerosis or ALS, a progressive disease of the nervous system that affects nerve cells in the brain and spinal cord, causing loss of muscle control. The disease is often called Lou Gehrig's disease, after the famous baseball player who died from it. ALS is a horrible illness. The motor function of the central nervous system is destroyed, but the mind remains fully aware until the end.

ALS drained the life from every muscle in Carl Smith's body. I was amazed at the love that Barbara showed as she attended to her husband. She did for him what mothers do for infants. She bathed, fed, and dressed him. Night and day, she tenderly hovered over him. If she complained, I never heard it. If she frowned, I never saw it. What I heard and saw was someone who kept their promise to "love in sickness and in health." "This is what love does," her actions declared as she shaved his face, washed his body, and changed his sheets.

Love is an action verb. In other words, love is shown in deliberate action. That is the same love that God has for you.

Today, most people are filled with many romantic illusions about love.

> ## Hosea
>
> **From the Hebrew name עָשׂוֹה_ (Hoshe'a) meaning "salvation"**

They believe that love has nothing to do with our will. Instead, we are just overwhelmed by love and follow whatever course it leads. However, the Bible teaches that love is largely a matter of will. That is why "We are not in love anymore" is not a valid reason to end a marriage.

In the Book of Hosea, God used the relationship between Hosea, and his wife, Gomer, as a living illustration of God's love. Why any parents would name their daughter Gomer, I do not know, but that is her name. Each time I read her name; I am reminded of the character on "The Andy Griffith Show." Do you remember Gomer Pyle? "Shazam!" "Golly." "Sur-prise, sur-prise, sur-prise." But don't get sidetracked by her name. I mean, I doubt seriously that she looked anything at all like Jim Nabors.

Anyway, in the story, Gomer leaves Hosea high and dry to go after other lovers. The Bible teaches that the way Gomer treats Hosea is a picture of Israel's treatment of God. Just like Gomer was

> ## Did You Know?
>
> **Some scholars believe the name "Gomer" may have been a prophetic statement relating to the future place of Jewish slavery. Her name seems to correspond with Germany—the offspring of Gomer listed in the table of nations in Genesis 10. Could her name be a prophecy of Germany—the place of Jewish slavery—from which the house of Israel was to be redeemed?**

unfaithful in her marriage, Israel was unfaithful to God. The Bible says that unfaithfulness to God by His people is considered by God to be adultery.

The Bible also says that Hosea had every right to get a divorce. He could have said, "It's over. She cheated on me, so I'll just go my way and she can just go hers." But that is not the way God loves. Instead, God told Hosea his wife was in town being auctioned off as a slave, and he should go pay his hard-earned money to buy her back. God told Hosea to take his wife back and love her. The relationship between Hosea and Gomer is a picture of God's love for Israel. Regardless of how Israel rejected God, He never stopped loving them. That is the theme of the Book of Hosea.

Yet, there is another theme in the book of Hosea. It is a message that speaks to us today. It is a message of unconditional love. It is a message that shows us God loves the unlovely.

Relationships

Hosea's prophetic ministry to the Northern Kingdom occurred "in the days of Uzziah, Jotham, Ahaz, and Hezekiah, kings of Judah, and in the days of Jeroboam the son of Joash, king of Israel" (Hosea 1:1). At that same time, the prophet Isaiah was addressing the Southern Kingdom. Hosea was also a contemporary of Amos. Both prophets were sent to the Northern Kingdom and began their ministries a few years before Isaiah.

> ### Date
>
> **Hosea's prophecies were proclaimed in the Northern Kingdom of Israel between 750–725 B.C.**

Hosea wrote around 750 B.C. Israel was under the rule of Jeroboam II. Although peace and apparent prosperity reigned, judgment and chaos were just around the corner. During Hosea's lifetime kings, priests, and all their aristocratic supporters abandoned the ways of the Lord and instead followed the idolatrous ways of the Canaanites. Religion was booming—but it was the religion of the fertility cults involving all kinds of sexual excess and perversion. Assyria loomed as the executor of the Lord's judgment on a rebellious and adulterous people. In 733, just seventeen years after this writing, Israel was broken up by the Assyrians.

God used Hosea's life as a living sermon to speak about relationships—specifically the relationship of marriage. The first chapter opens with God telling Hosea to get married. Normally, that would be a good thing, but God tells His prophet to marry a prostitute. The Bible does not sugarcoat it; she was a whore. She offered sex to men in exchange for money.

Soon after they were married, Gomer began to have children. God told Hosea to give very unusual names to the children. The firstborn was named *Jezreel* which means "the valley of destruction." The second child was named *Loruhamah* meaning "no mercy." The third kid was given the name *Loammi* which means "not my people." God told Hosea to name these children in such a way to describe His current feelings toward His people. They had turned their back on Him and had been unfaithful. So, God was about to bring destruction, have no mercy, and, as far as He was concerned, they were not His people.

Did You Know?

The love that Hosea describes is the Hebrew *hesed*. It conveys the idea of a covenant or loyalty. *Hesed* is steadfast, committed love.

At first, it seems Hosea had a good relationship with Gomer. However, somewhere along the way, she returned to her old life of prostitution. She abandoned her husband and family. She became unlovely.

The Bible does not tell us why she left. Perhaps Gomer thought like many people do today. Maybe she thought, "I deserve more than this! I deserve to be happy! I deserve a better life!" But here is the truth: you don't deserve to be happy. You deserve Hell. But Jesus came to save you from Hell. God didn't give you what you deserve, and marriage isn't about what you deserve either. It is about commitment.

One day, a young man came to my office for counseling. As we talked, he said, "I just don't love my wife anymore." I said, "Well, just go love her." He didn't understand that love is an action verb. He looked at me and frowned. Then he went on to say he was no longer physically attracted to his wife. As I listened, I came to understand he never really loved his wife. Instead, he lusted for his wife.

Today, many people marry for lust. Sadly, physical desire fades. If you marry for lust, you will likely end up divorced. Instead, marry for commitment.

Aren't you glad God does not love you the way some people love their spouses today?

Redemption

Hosea's story is also a story of redemption. After Gomer left, Hosea's days were filled with taking care of three children. His nights were filled with loneliness as he reached for her on the empty side of the bed. Then one day news reaches Hosea that the woman he loves has become a slave.

So I bought her to me for fifteen pieces of silver, and for an homer of barley, and an half homer of barley.

—Hosea 3:2

In the time of Hosea, there were three ways in which a person could become a slave. First was by conquest. An army could invade the land and take you captive and make you a slave. Second, you could be born a slave. Your parents were slaves, and you were born into slavery. Third, you could become a slave by debt. This is what happened to Gomer. She had become a slave because she could not pay her debts, so they were auctioning her off to pay the debt.

Gomer was a woman on the auction block because she had a debt she could not pay. It was a debt so large, she was not able to satisfy it. Left to herself, she was a slave. Left to herself, she was doomed.

In those days, when they auctioned off a slave, it was a humiliating experience. The slave was stripped naked and put on a platform for everyone to see. All her clothes were removed so the buyers could see the merchandise.

I want you to understand that not only is Gomer a picture of unfaithful Israel, but she is also a picture of people without Jesus Christ. If you have not received Christ as Savior and Lord, she is a picture of you. You have run up a debt that you cannot pay. You are a sinner, and you owe a debt for your sins. There is nothing you have and nothing you can do to satisfy that debt. Just like that woman who stands there naked before everybody in town, you stand naked and condemned before a Holy God. You are stripped bare, doomed, and hopeless.

What is it that moves Hosea to leave his house when he finds out his wife is on the auction block of sin? It's love. There was unconditional love in his heart. And that is the nature and the heart of God. God loves you in spite of your unlovely sin.

Can you imagine the scene? Hosea walked through the streets toward the auction. People said, "I heard about your wife! I heard she got what she deserved. I bet you are going there to have the last laugh. I bet she regrets the day she left you."

As he drew closer, Hosea heard the voice of the auctioneer. The auctioneer shouted, "We have a woman here! Her name is Gomer! Her profession is a prostitute! Is there anyone willing to pay the price?"

Understand that Hosea did not owe the debt, but he had the fifteen pieces of silver and the half bushel of barley to pay the price. Gomer did not deserve to be redeemed and set free. Still, Hosea, because of his unconditional love, stepped up to bid.

Imagine the scene for a moment. Imagine Hosea bearing the indignity of entering a crowd of men who gazed at his undressed wife. If that was not enough, he also had to bid for her. One man yelled, "Five shekels!" Another shouted, "Six!" Hosea screamed, "Seven shekels!" Another man bellowed, "Eight!" Hosea screamed, "Nine!" The man shot back, "Eleven shekels!" Hosea cried, "Twelve!" The other man yelled, "Thirteen!" Hosea didn't have much left! So, he raised his voice, "Fifteen shekels of silver and a half of bushel of barley!" The auctioneer said, "Sold to the highest bidder!"

I imagine Hosea helped his naked wife down from the auction block, took off his robe, and put it around her. Then he spoke to Gomer:

And I said unto her, Thou shalt abide for me many days; thou shalt not play the harlot, and thou shalt not be for another man: so will I also be for thee.

—Hosea 3:3

It was as if Hosea said, "I bought you back because you are my wife; because I am committed to you. No matter what you have done, no matter how far you have fallen, I still love you. I paid the price so you and I could be together. You are going to be faithful to me and I am going to be faithful to you."

There comes a point in the life of every sinner where you are on the auction block of sin. You are doomed. The devil says, "I've got you and nobody can pay the price!" But through the crowd comes One named Jesus. He says, "I will pay your sin debt." He says, "I will robe you in my righteousness."

Jesus paid the price to redeem you from the chains of sin, but He did not redeem you for you to go out and play the harlot anymore. He redeemed you so you could live as a changed person, and He demands your faithfulness because you were bought and paid for with His precious blood.

And on the day that you put your faith and trust in Jesus, the chains fell away. You're not a slave to the devil. You're not a slave to sin. You're not a slave to cocaine. You're not a slave to Jack Daniels. You're not a slave to pornography.

You're not a slave to the love of money. You're not a slave to pride. You have been set free by the glorious grace of God because Jesus paid it all and He paid it in full. He paid the price in spite of your unlovely sin.

Renewal

Hosea's story also speaks of renewal. There is a prophecy in Hosea 3 that looks forward to the renewal of God's people.

> **For the children of Israel shall abide many days without a king, and without a prince, and without a sacrifice, and without an image, and without an ephod, and without teraphim.**
>
> —Hosea 3:4

Hosea delivered a message, a prophecy, of what was going to someday happen to the nation of Israel. He said Israel would be a long time without a king. We are living in that day now. Today, no king is sitting on the throne in Israel.

Hosea also said Israel would be a long time without a temple or priests. The temple was destroyed in A.D. 70. There is no temple in Israel today.

> **Afterward shall the children of Israel return, and seek the Lord their God, and David their king; and shall fear the Lord and his goodness in the latter days.**
>
> —Hosea 3:5

However, Hosea predicted that a day

Did You Know?

Hosea ended his predictions in chapter 14 by delivering God's promise to restore Israel once again. He likened the final restoration of Israel to a flourishing olive tree. Israel will ultimately be purged of its sin and experience God's full forgiveness and restoration under the coming Messiah.

was coming when the children of Israel would return and seek the Lord their God and David. He was speaking of One who will rule in David's place—who would be from the royal line of David.

Hosea also said Israel would fear God in the "latter days." That speaks of the future kingdom when God will gather His children and Jesus Christ will rule from the throne of David forever and ever.

Sometimes, God's people are unfaithful. Sometimes, God's people stop praying. Sometimes, God's people stop reading His Word. Sometimes, God's people skip church.

If you have been unfaithful to God, just like Hosea wanted his wife back, God wants you back. God is calling you back to Him. God says, "Come back to Me. I understand that you've wandered. You've gotten deep into sin. You've replaced Me with something else!" But God also softly and tenderly says, "Come home." God loves you in spite of the ugliness of your sin.

There is one final thing I want you to notice in Hosea's story. Notice that Hosea gave Gomer no condemnation. He just said, "I want you to come home and I want you to be with me." He just put his arm around her and said, "I've forgotten about the past." That is exactly what God says to the Christian who has fallen into sin. God says, "I'm right where you left Me! If you'll come back, we will start over again!" God forgets all about your ugliness and loves you anyway.

God loves the unlovely.

She was fifteen, he was seventeen when they met. All through high school, they dated. After graduation, it was not a surprise when they got married.

> ### Did You Know?
>
> **The book of Hosea illustrates that no one is beyond the offer of our forgiveness because no one sits outside God's offer of forgiveness. Certainly, God brings judgment on those who turn from Him, but Hosea's powerful act of restoration within his marriage sets the bar high for those of us seeking godliness in our lives.**

Four years later, she stood in her kitchen with a stack of dirty dishes in the sink, two children at her feet, and a pile of dirty diapers in the corner. Tears streamed down her face. This was not the life she expected. Depressed and disappointed, she took off her apron and walked out.

She called that night, and her young husband answered the phone. He was, understandably, quite worried and, also, quite angry. "Where are you?" he asked, his concern and his anger fighting for control of his voice. "How are the children?" she asked, ignoring his question. "Well, if you mean, have they been fed, they have. I also put them to bed. They are wondering, just as I am, where are you? What are you doing?" She hung up the phone that night, but it wasn't the last of the phone calls.

She called almost every week for the next three months. Her husband, knowing something was seriously wrong, began, in those phone calls, to plead with her to come home. He would tell her that the children were with their grandparents during the day and were well cared for. He would tell her he loved her. He would tell her how much they all missed her and then he would try to find out where she was. Whenever the conversation turned to her whereabouts, she would hang up.

Finally, the young husband could stand it no longer. He took their savings and hired a private detective to find his wife. The detective reported that the runaway wife was in a third-rate hotel in Des Moines, Iowa.

The young man borrowed the money from his in-laws, bought a plane ticket, and flew to Des Moines. After taking a cab from the airport to the hotel, he climbed the stairs to his wife's room on the third floor.

If you had been there, you would have seen the doubt in his eyes and you would have noticed the perspiration on his forehead. His hand trembled as he knocked on the door. When his wife opened the door, he forgot his prepared speech and said, "I love you so much. Won't you please come home?" She fell in his arms. They went home together.

One evening some weeks later, the children were in bed and he and his wife were sitting in the living room in front of the fire. He finally got up enough courage to ask the question that had haunted him for so many months. He asked, "Why wouldn't you come home? Why, when I told you repeatedly that I loved you and missed you, didn't you come home?" She said, "Because, before those were only words. But then you came. You came."

Love is an action verb. The young man put his love into action, and he came to Des Moines for his wife. Hosea put his love into action, and he came to the auction block for Gomer. Jesus put His love into action, and He came to this world for you.

No matter what you have done; no matter how unlovable you have become; God loves you.

God loves the unlovely.

Come home to Him today.

A Moment of Prophecy

In Chapter 2 of the Book of Hosea, God predicts the return of Israel to their land.

> *Therefore, behold, I will allure her, and bring her into the wilderness, and speak comfortably unto her. And I will give her vineyards from thence, and the valley of Achor for a door of hope: and she shall sing there, as in the days of her youth, and as in the day when she came up out of the land of Egypt. And it shall be at that day, saith the LORD, that thou shalt call me Ishi; and shalt call me no more Baali.*
>
> — Hosea 2:14–16

After 2,000 years of being in exile, God has lured the Jews back to their land. When they arrived, it was a wilderness. Today, it is a land of agricultural abundance. The people of Israel have reclaimed the Jordan River valley—the historic valley of Achor. This valley was the entryway into the Promised Land following their exodus from Egypt. Once again, the Jewish people have turned their land into a "door of hope."

Someday soon, this prophecy will be completely fulfilled when God's people call Him *Ishi* (my husband), and they no longer call him *Baali* (my master).

CHAPTER 2

Restoring the Years

And I will restore to you the years that the locust hath eaten, the cankerworm, and the caterpiller, and the palmerworm, my great army which I sent among you.

—Joel 2:25

One year, when my daughter, Abby, was four years old, we bought her a Barbie Dreamhouse for Christmas. On Christmas Eve, after the kids had gone to bed, my wife said, "Honey, you have to stay up and put Abby's dollhouse together." I said, "Okay," and she went to bed.

When you buy a new tool, appliance, or even a Barbie Dreamhouse, you will always find one thing accompanying the new item—a manual. The manual is there to instruct you as to what pieces are inside, how to assemble the doohickey, and how to operate it.

Now, I am a grown man. I don't need a manual. Because I am a man, I instinctively know how to put things together. All I ever do is look at the picture on the front of the box and put the item together. I looked at the picture on the Barbie Dreamhouse box and thought, "Looks simple enough." So, I opened the box and dumped the contents. Seven hundred small plastic pieces spilled out onto the floor. I thought, "It's going to be a long night."

I assembled the dollhouse and after about two hours, I felt like it was finished. Somehow, I ended up with a few extra pieces. Also, the elevator did not go all the way to the top. Please, no comments about my elevator also not going all the way to the top. I tried to fix the elevator and install the missing pieces. Two more hours passed, and I still had not fixed the elevator or discovered where the mystery pieces fit. It was late and I was starting to get tired and frustrated.

Finally, I decided to get the manual out to look and see if the manufacturer had included some extra pieces just in case you happen to lose one. To my surprise, the manual was written in Chinese. I searched through the extra pieces, the packing, and the box until I found another manual in English. Of course, according to the manual, there were not supposed to be extra pieces.

After five minutes of reading the manual, I realized I missed several important steps which would have been helpful to know about four hours ago. I ended up tearing it apart and starting over by using the manual. I would have saved myself a headache and gotten a good night's sleep if I would have just looked at it in the first place.

In life, we often make the wrong choices without consulting the Manual—the Holy Bible. Sometimes our own bad choices make a complete mess of our lives. One of my favorite quotes is from legendary movie actor John Wayne, who once said, "Life is hard; it's even harder if you're stupid." In other words, life is tough enough without making it worse with bad decisions.

> ## Joel
>
> From the Hebrew name יוֹאֵל (Yo'el) meaning "YAHWEH is God"

Do you feel like you have made a mess of your life? Do you feel like your life is too messed up to ever fix? Do you feel like your life is a disaster?

The book of Joel describes a disaster. Disaster had come to the Southern Kingdom of Judah and its capital, Jerusalem. A dark cloud of locusts descended upon the country and destroyed the crops. The locusts stripped away every bit of vegetation. The people could have fought against a human enemy, but they had no defense against this swarm of chewing, devouring, destructive locusts.

The locusts were God's judgment upon Judah's sin. Sin always brings judgment. Sin always brings misery. Sin always brings destruction. Like devouring locusts, sin will lay waste to your life and will strip away everything good from you.

Someone is reading this, and you have allowed sin to control your thinking process. You have allowed sin to control your will. You have allowed sin to control you and you have made a series of disastrous choices over your life. Because of those bad choices, your life has been laid waste by the locusts of Satan's destructive power.

What was your bad choice? Alcohol? Drugs? A series of failed relationships? One horrible financial decision after another? An abortion? Homosexuality? Adultery? Looking at pornography? Or a combination of bad choices?

Everybody makes bad choices—even Christians. God's people often walk in the flesh. Sometimes we stop allowing the promptings of the Holy Spirit to guide our life. Sometimes we make choices outside of the will of God that drive us down a path of waste.

Date

Because Joel does not mention any Jewish or gentile kings, nor does he refer to any well-known historical events in his prophecies, dating his book is difficult. Since the Hebrew ordering of the books of the Bible puts Joel between Hosea and Amos, many scholars date the book to an early date of about 835–796 B.C. Other scholars place Joel much later between 500–350 B.C. The date is not as important as his message. The country of Judah was going through a disaster. He was focused on the disaster at hand, and not on where he fits into the timeline of history.

Do you ever look back on your life and feel like your future is doomed by your past? You have wasted your time. You have wasted your talents. You have wasted your emotions. You have wasted your health. You have wasted the best days of your life and you feel like your future will be filled with failure. When you look in the rearview mirror, failure is all you see. Sin has laid waste to your life.

So, what does God have to say? What does God have to say to someone who has wasted their life? We find the answer in this book by the prophet Joel.

> ## Did You Know?
>
> **The Apostle Peter, under the inspiration of the Holy Spirit, quoted Joel (Acts 2:16–21) indicating that the prophecies were not fulfilled in his day but must await the time of the Last Days Tribulation.**

Joel was a man who was willing to say to the Southern Kingdom that God will not be ignored by His people who tend to forget Him sometimes.

In fact, Joel's name means "the Lord is God!" Joel's message, life, ministry, and even his name was to remind the people that the Lord is God. Now, I cannot think of a more relevant message for this busy day in which we live. We are so busy that we don't have time for God. We are busy working two jobs to afford to put in that swimming pool. We are busy driving around in our gas-guzzling cars. We are busy going to Starbucks to get a double caramel vanilla whipped mocha frappuccino latte with sprinkles and an extra shot. We are busy binge-watching shows on Netflix. We are so busy we forget there is a God who wants to have a personal relationship with us.

God is willing to use any means necessary to remove distractions to get us to turn to Him. Joel describes a terrible plague of locusts that destroyed the nation. There is a price to be paid when people rebel against God.

Yet Joel also speaks of grace. Joel comes out thundering judgment and breathing fire, but he ends up speak-

> ## Did You Know?
>
> **Joel most likely wrote his book somewhere around 830 B.C. As a young man, he might have known Elijah, and in later years he would have been a contemporary of Elisha.**

ing of the love, mercy, and tenderness of God. Even though God is holy, just, and righteous, He is still a God of grace who came down here and clothed Himself in the Person of Jesus Christ. While Jesus was here, He went home and ate with people that society had rejected. Jesus even took the time to help a woman who was caught in the very act of adultery restore her life. The Lord always had time for the lowest of the low.

So, if you think you have made so many bad choices in your life that God has forgotten you, you are wrong. God has not forgotten you. God doesn't throw away broken things. He doesn't abandon people who mess up. He restores and salvages.

Back in June of 1985, a man from the Soviet Union visited an art gallery in Amsterdam. The man walked up to a very famous painting by Rembrandt called "Danae." In an insane frenzy, he attacked the priceless painting. He threw sulfuric acid on the canvas and cut it twice with a knife.

The painting was ruined. Where there was once a beautiful work of art, there was now a mixture of spots, cuts, and dripping paint. The masterpiece was ruined. However, the art gallery did not throw Rembrandt's painting away. Instead, they called in experts, and they did everything in their power to restore the painting to its former glory.

I don't know what kind of mess you have made of your life, but the Great Artist on high, the Lord Jesus Christ, does not throw away damaged people. He does not throw away broken lives. He won't just restore you to what you ought to be. He will make you what you never were for His glory and your good.

Ruin

That which the palmerworm hath left hath the locust eaten; and that which the locust hath left hath the cankerworm eaten; and that which the cankerworm hath left hath the caterpiller eaten.

—Joel 1:4

The Book of Joel opens with a description of a natural catastrophe. An army of locusts came from the north and devoured and ate the crops in the Southern Kingdom of Judah. The fields were stripped bare. There was nothing to eat. A famine followed. People were starving. The nation was in a mess, and God Almighty said they did not have anybody to blame but themselves.

Several years ago, a prominent televangelist was caught in a scandal. He was accused of taking money from his ministry and having an affair with a secretary. I remember seeing an interview with that man right before he got sent to prison. In the interview, he said, "I can't believe what God is doing to me!" God didn't do that to him. He did it to himself. We often blame God for something we did ourselves.

Have you ever said, "I can't believe what God is doing to me?" God didn't do anything. You did it to yourself. Most of the time, the devil doesn't even have to mess with us because we do enough damage on our own with our own bad choices.

Joel says that is the reason the locusts came. Wave after wave of locusts came, and different kinds of locusts came until there was nothing left standing. Nothing could be salvaged. The people couldn't stop the locusts. They couldn't produce crops. They were in a hopeless situation.

What did the people of Judah do to cause locusts to come down and devastate them? Joel, speaking for God, answers:

And ye shall know that I am in the midst of Israel, and that I am the LORD your God, and *none else*: and my people shall never be ashamed.

—Joel 2:27

The people violated the First Commandment. They put another god before God. They worshipped idols. You probably are thinking, "I don't worship idols. I have never bowed down to an image made of wood or stone." That may be true, but we have different idols today. An idol is anything that comes before

God. Today, we have replaced God with our dreams and desires. We have replaced Him with possessions and pleasures.

When I was sixteen, I had a crush on a girl named Dixie who did not have the best reputation. To be honest, Dixie had no morals or redeeming qualities at all other than the fact that she was pretty. My wife might read this, so let me say that my wife is ten million times prettier than Dixie. Anyway, I knew she was trouble, but I asked Dixie out anyway. My Aunt Gayle found out that I was going out with Dixie, and she said, "Have you lost your ever-loving mind!" When we do what we want and not what God wants, He says, "Have you lost your ever-loving mind!"

Sometimes God sends locusts. He sends locusts and they devour our finances. He sends locusts and they strip our possessions. He sends locusts and they devastate our families. He sends locusts and they destroy our health. Then, when we are stripped bare, we need to understand the purpose of the locusts is to get us to come to our senses and to get us to say, "Maybe it would be wise if I put God first and stop calling the shots myself."

Restoration

You may be saying, "Yes, I've made some bad choices. I've made some stupid decisions." You may be wondering if there is any hope for things to turn around in your life. Yes, there is hope. God speaks of restoration.

> **And I will restore to you the years that the locust hath eaten, the canker-worm, and the caterpiller, and the palmerworm, my great army which I sent among you.**
>
> —Joel 2:25

God does not say, "I might" or "I may." He says, "I *will* restore to you ..." You can't undo the past, but you can redeem the life you have wasted. You can't go back and live those wasted years again, but God can restore the life you have now and give you a better future. Today, if you'll make God your top priority, God will work in a mighty way. He will give you healed relationships. He will give you new friends. He will break the power of sin in your life. He will restore your joy and happiness.

I saw a recent news story on television about the restoration of a World War II Hurricane fighter plane. The news reporter asked the restorer, "Is this plane as good as new?" The restorer answered, "No, it is better than new."

Let Jesus restore you and you will be better than new.

Revival

There is also a promise in Joel of revival. It is no coincidence that in the book of Acts on the Day of Pentecost Peter preached from this very text in Joel to start the greatest revival in history.

> **Be glad then, ye children of Zion, and rejoice in the LORD your God: for he hath given you the former rain moderately, and he will cause to come down for you the rain, the former rain, and the latter rain in the first month.** —Joel 2:23

The "former rain" was the rain that came between October and November. The "latter rain" was the rain that came between March and April. The former rain was when the seed was planted. The latter rain would bring the fields to ripeness so the crops could be harvested. This was the promise of revival. God said the former rain will give way to a future rain. God wants to send an old-fashioned Holy Ghost revival in your heart, in your church, in your community, and in this country.

This country is in desperate need of revival. We need revival to get us back to our first love, Jesus. We need revival to understand our purpose. Today, most people tragically walk through this world without purpose.

Several years ago, there was a young man who went to see his uncle who was a preacher in Georgia. He walked into his uncle's study and asked, "What are you going to preach over this Sunday?" His uncle said, "Son, I'm going to preach on this verse from the Gospel of John—John 18:37 where Jesus said, "For this cause I was born, and for this cause I have come into the world." The young man was quiet for a moment. Then he asked, "Why was I born? Why am I here?" The pastor said, "If you obey God, He will show you why you were born."

The young man left his uncle's study. He walked down the street and he saw and heard a crowd gathering in front of the theater. He ran down to see what the commotion was about. The theater was on fire and people were trapped inside. The young man entered the burning theater and rescued one man. He ran back in and brought out another. He ran back inside repeatedly until he brought out thirteen people.

When the young man rescued thirteen people, a falling timber hit him on the head and knocked him unconscious. He was severely burned, but he was rescued by firemen. He was rushed to the hospital. The news of the young man's condition reached his uncle, and he hurried to his bedside. Just before he died, the young man regained consciousness for one last moment. At that moment, he looked at his uncle and said, "Now, I know why I was born. For this cause, I came into the world. I came to save those thirteen people."

You are not reading this by accident. You are not reading this by fate. God has a purpose for you. If you are a believer in Jesus Christ, you can have revival. You can realize I'm not here for me. You can realize I'm here to serve Jesus. You can realize I'm here to serve others.

Regeneration

And it shall come to pass, that whosoever shall call on the name of the LORD shall be delivered ...

—Joel 2:32a

If you are not a believer in Jesus Christ, you do not need revival. You need regeneration. You must be born again. The Bible says whoever calls on the name of the Lord shall be saved. It doesn't matter who you are or what you've done, the Lord wants to give you a second chance. You may have started this day going to Hell, but you can end it going to Heaven. You can call on Jesus today and be saved. Jesus can restore the years.

> ### Did You Know?
>
> The Book of Joel ends with verses that describe the Millennial Kingdom as a place where Judah and Jerusalem will dwell in peace forever under the rule of the Messiah.

Many years ago, a wealthy businessman from Chicago went to Kentucky on vacation. There, he met a beautiful southern belle. There was instant chemistry and they fell in love.

The businessman romanced the Kentucky girl, and they were married. He took her back to Chicago and they lived in a palace—a mansion. For three wonderful years, they lived in the palace. They were happy and in love. It was almost Heaven on Earth.

One day, she had a violent and painful seizure. It was so severe, it caused her to lose her mind. On her best days, she was slightly demented. Most days, she was a raving maniac. Her wild screams were so bloodcurdling that the neighbors complained. Her husband hired the best doctors and specialists, but none could help. Friends and family said, "You've got to have her committed. She's crazy!" He said, "I just can't do that. I love her too much."

Finally, a doctor suggested, "Try taking her back to Kentucky. Take her back to her home. I think seeing familiar things will help to bring her out of her madness." So, the businessman took her back to the bluegrass lands of Kentucky. He drove her down to the creek where she played as a little girl and where they had courted three years earlier. She looked at familiar wildflowers. She smelled familiar smells. She experienced all the sights and sounds of her childhood. However, it didn't seem to help. All he saw in her eyes was wild insanity.

So, disappointed and heartbroken, he loaded her up and headed back to Chicago. When they got home, he lifted her out of the car and carried her up the steps when her head dropped. Her head slumped on his shoulder. He carried her up to their bedroom and gently placed her on the bed. She had fallen into a deep sleep. She had not had natural sleep in a long time. Most of the time, she was so restless that she had to be drugged.

Her husband thought, "She looks so peaceful. Maybe she'll wake up in an hour." So, he sat there beside her bed and watched her as she slept. An hour passed. Then two. Then three. He sat there all night long.

When the sun came up, the light came into the window and fell across her face. As he watched, her eyelids fluttered. She blinked and a little smile came across her lips. She looked up at her husband and he couldn't believe it—the madness had left her eyes. The insanity, the wildness was gone. She sat up and said, "Honey, I've been on a long, long, long journey. What have you been doing?" He looked at her through tears of joy and said, "I've been waiting for you. I've been waiting for you."

From generation to generation, God is the same. No matter what distance there is between you and Jesus, He is waiting on you. Open your eyes to Him and let Him restore the years.

A Moment of Prophecy

Joel used the occasion of an actual devastating plague of locusts as a prophetic type. Joel warned the people that God's judgment would certainly fall and leave the nation of Judah desolate. The Apostle John picked up on the prophecies of Joel when he described the invasion of a mighty army in Revelation 9.

CHAPTER 3

The Silence of God

Behold, the days come, saith the Lord GOD, that I will send a famine in the land, not a famine of bread, nor a thirst for water, but of hearing the words of the LORD: And they shall wander from sea to sea, and from the north even to the east, they shall run to and fro to seek the word of the LORD, and shall not find it.

—Amos 8:11–12

One time, a married couple were having some problems at home. They fussed and argued for several days. Eventually, they were so aggravated, they started giving each other the silent treatment. For about a week, they didn't say a word to each other.

While they were in the middle of the silent treatment, the husband planned a fishing trip with his brothers. He was supposed to meet them early on a Saturday morning. He realized that he would need his wife to wake him up at 5:00 a.m. for him to meet his brothers for their fishing trip. However, he didn't want to be the first to

> ## Amos
>
> From the Hebrew עָמַס (amas) meaning "load or burden"

break the silence. That would mean he would be the loser of the argument. So, he got an idea. He took a sheet of paper, and he wrote "Please wake me up at 5:00 a.m." Then he pinned the note to his wife's pillow on her side of the bed.

The next morning, he woke, only to find out that it was 7:30. He overslept and missed his fishing trip. He was furious and was about to go and see why his wife didn't wake him up when he noticed a piece of paper on the nightstand by his side of the bed. The paper said, "It is 5:00 am. Wake up!"

Nobody likes the silent treatment. If you make some people mad, they will not speak to you. You can say, "Good morning," "Hello," or "How's it going?" and they will not answer you. They will not acknowledge you. Oh, they will talk about you behind your back to anyone that will listen, but they will not talk to you. They just give you the silent treatment.

> ### Date
>
> Because Amos mentions an earthquake (Amos 1:1) and a solar eclipse (Amos 8:9), scholars date his writing at 763 B.C.

And it's bad enough when people give you the silent treatment, but even worse is the silence of God. In the book of Amos, God said that He was going to send a famine of hearing the words of God. He would give His people the silent treatment.

The man God used to send this unusual message wasn't a traditional prophet, priest, or preacher. Amos was a country farmer. We find out a little about his background in Amos chapter 7.

> **Then answered Amos, and said to Amaziah, I was no prophet, neither was I a prophet's son; but I was an herdman, and a gatherer of sycamore fruit: And the LORD took me as I followed the flock, and the LORD said unto me, Go, prophesy unto my people Israel.**
>
> —Amos 7:14–15

Amos did not have the credentials of a traditional prophet. He never went to school. His family members were not prophets. He was a sheepherder and a tender of sycamore trees.

The sycamore trees he tended were not the same kind of sycamore trees we have in America today. The sycamore trees in the Near East were fruit-bearing trees. The fruit of the sycamore looked something like a fig. To make the fruit tasty and edible, the man who tended the tree had to pinch the fruit. By pinching the fruit, he bruised the fruit. When harvest time came, the pinched and bruised fruit tasted delicious.

"A Divided People"
Map of Ancient
Israel & Judah

So, before God called Amos, his life was filled with exciting days of cleaning up after sheep; running off wolves; and pinching and bruising fruit in a grove of sycamore trees. He was a country boy—a farmer that God called to the ministry. He reminds me a lot of … me. I identify with him. Like Amos, I'm just a country boy. I didn't go to the best schools. I don't come from a line of preachers. I don't have the best pastoral credentials. I'm just a man God called to leave the country and take the saving Gospel of Jesus Christ to a lost and dying world. So, I feel a kinship to Amos.

Amos lived in the Southern Kingdom of Judah. After King Solomon died, there was a civil war. The nation was divided in half. The Northern Kingdom was called Israel and the Southern kingdom was called Judah. The Northern Kingdom had as its center of worship a place called Bethel. There was a great church or cathedral, so to speak, built in Bethel. It was the national church because the king worshiped there. In the Southern Kingdom of Judah, the center of worship was Jerusalem. Why would God send a preacher from the Southern Kingdom of Judah to the Northern Kingdom of Israel? Because there was no one righteous in the north. In Amos 7:15 we read, "And the LORD took me as I followed the flock, and the LORD said unto me, Go, prophesy unto my people Israel." One day, Amos was tending his sheep when God called him to preach to the Northern Kingdom of Israel.

A Strange Starvation

Behold, the days come, saith the Lord GOD, that I will send a famine in the land, not a famine of bread, nor a thirst for water, but of hearing the words of the LORD.

—Amos 8:11

Amos spoke of a strange starvation. He spoke of a famine—not a famine of food or water, but a famine of hearing the Word of God.

The people of Amos' time knew about famines. They had been through a few. They knew what it was like to live through a drought and watch one crop after another fail and die. They understood the suffering famine brings when people starve to death.

However, God said He would send a different kind of famine. God said He was going to send a famine more devastating than the kind where you hunger for bread or thirst for water. God would send a famine of hearing the words of the Lord. God will be silent.

In the Gospel of Matthew, Jesus said, "Man shall not live by bread alone, but by every word that proceedeth out of the mouth of God" (Matthew 4:4). For you to grow spiritually, you must feast on the words of the Bible. If you don't eat the meat of the Word, if you don't drink the milk of the Word, then you won't be spiritually strong. Every kind of life requires nutrients—including your spirit. God gave you a Bible. God gave you men who have the gift of preaching and teaching. God gave you the privilege to hear the Word of God.

Are you listening?

At this point in history, God had sent prophet after prophet, preacher after preacher, messenger after messenger. Still, God's people would not listen. So, God says the Word would cease. God would go silent. He would send a famine—a famine of the heart. God would send a famine of hearing the Word of God.

One of the ministries of the Holy Spirit is to draw men to Jesus. You cannot be saved unless the Spirit of God convicts, draws, and regenerates you. When you hear the Word of God, the Holy Spirit convicts and draws you to Christ for you to be saved. However, there is a line out there. Each time you say no to Jesus, you move closer to that line. Eventually, there will come a day when you cross that line, and the Gospel will not affect you anymore. Your heart will be hardened.

You may be thinking, "I'm young. I've got forty years to live." That may be true, but if you do live forty years, you may cross that line before you die. Then you will never have a chance to be saved in this world or in the world to come. You will have gone too far. You have said no to God one time too many. When the Word of God is preached, you will not hear it. You may hear it with your ears, but not with your heart.

If you are reading this and you are not a believer in Jesus Christ, there will come a day when God deals with you for the last time. Then you will never have another opportunity to be saved again. Don't put it off. Give your life to Christ now.

Back in 1899, a group of men went to Alaska to make their fortune mining for gold. They set out to find land to stake their claim. After several weeks of travel, they made it into the interior when they came upon a miner's hut. The hut seemed to be abandoned, so they went inside.

Inside, they found two skeletons and a large quantity of gold. On a table, next to the gold, they found a letter. The letter detailed the two men's successful hunt for gold. When they discovered gold, they put off going back into town for winter supplies. They were so focused on digging out more gold that they continued to put off going into town for supplies. Each day, they found more gold. Each day, they were so eager to get more gold that they put off going to town for supplies.

One morning, the men woke up to find a great snowstorm blowing down on them. The snow fell for several days. It became deeper and deeper. Soon, there was no way out. All their food eventually ran out. Then the men lay down in the middle of all their gold and died. They had put off going for supplies one time too many.

Today, you might be focused on the things of this world. You want money, houses, land, and more stuff. You are so focused on the things of this world that you have put off preparing for the coming world. If you are not careful, you can put it off one time too many.

Are you hearing what God is saying to your heart?

God sent the famine in the time of Amos because the people were not listening. Consequently, God said, "If you don't want to hear what I've got to say, then silence is coming." God sent Amos to say, "There is a famine coming."

Amos is a great example of the kind of person God uses. He was an ordinary man. He had an ordinary job. He came from an ordinary family. Yet God still used him. God told Amos to go up to Bethel to a beautiful, prestigious, monumental church and preach.

God called a simple farmer to preach to a prosperous nation who had forgotten Him. You might think the financially flourishing times needed a sophisticated preacher—a smooth talker who graduated from a top theological seminary. But God had other plans. God knew He could use this unlikely man in a great way.

Perhaps it's time for you to start thinking outside the box. Perhaps you have thought God could only use you in ways that seem logical and reasonable. God can and will use you in ways that make sense, but you also need to think outside your box. The most important qualification is the call of God.

Is God calling you?

Amos was a southern backwater preacher. He probably ate fried chicken, grits, hominy, cornbread, and buttermilk. I am sure he had a glass of sweet tea in his hand. He was the kind of guy that would go around saying "ya'll" and "ain't." Instead of saying tomato, Amos would have said, "Ya'll ever had a mater sandwich?" Amos was a country preacher at best.

At first, the people in Bethel liked Amos. You will see why they liked him if you read his first chapter. They liked him at first because he preached against the sins of all the surrounding nations. Don't we all like to hear somebody preach when they are preaching about somebody else's sins? Amen, brother! Hallelujah! There's a bunch of heathens out there! But then Amos started preaching about their sins. Suddenly, the "amens" stopped and people squirmed in the pews.

Amos stood up and said to the Northern Kingdom of Israel, "You are prosperous. You've got money. But you've become greedy. Instead of using your money to help the poor, you are using the poor to make more money for yourselves. You are idol worshipers. Money has become your god. And I'm telling you that if you don't get right with God—God will send a famine. He's will send judgment. He's will send silence."

Amos was an old-fashioned, leather-lunged, peel the bark off the tree, rattle your cage, shuck the corn, shell the peas, thump the stump, hellfire, Holy Ghost preacher! He stood up and preached the truth and he didn't care who he offended. Sadly, nobody wanted to hear anybody like that then, and nobody wants to hear anybody like that today. We are too sophisticated to hear a plain word from God. We want somebody to tell us in a soft voice that everything in life is going to be rosy. We want somebody to preach prosperity to us. We say, "Leave me alone preacher. Mind your own business. Make me feel good."

Amos didn't say, "Something good is going to happen to you!" He didn't say, "You can climb every mountain!" He didn't say, "Problems are just possibilities!" He didn't say, "Just think positive!" He didn't say, "Follow every rainbow until you find your dreams!"

Amos preached the truth. Sometimes, the truth should make you feel bad. If the truth is you are disobedient to God, then you should feel bad. You should feel conviction. The job of a God-called preacher is not to make you feel good. His job is to deliver the Word of God and to tell you to get right with God.

> ### Did You Know?
>
> God says in Amos 2:5 that He will send "fire upon Judah, and it shall devour the palaces of Jerusalem." This prophecy was literally fulfilled in 586 B.C. when Jerusalem was destroyed by fire on the ninth of Av.

The Bible is full of good news. But how can you appreciate the good news if you don't hear the bad? The doctor comes out and he tells you that your sugar is out of whack—and you're a diabetic. That's the bad news. But then he tells you to take this medicine and you'll be fine. That's the good news.

I'm telling you today that there is a Hell and if you die without Jesus Christ, you will go there. That's the bad news. But you don't have to go to Hell—you can go to Heaven through the shed blood of our Lord Jesus Christ. That's the good news.

A Stubborn Sermonizer

Also Amaziah said unto Amos, O thou seer, go, flee thee away into the land of Judah, and there eat bread, and prophesy there: But prophesy not again any more at Bethel: for it is the king's chapel, and it is the king's court.

—Amos 7:12–13

Amos was a stubborn sermonizer. In other words, he was a hard-headed preacher. He didn't care about pleasing the crowd. Today, preachers are worried about pleasing crowds. Not Amos. He wasn't worried about crowds. He didn't have a lot of people following him around saying, "Could I get a copy of that message on CD?" or "Would you sign my Bible?"

Instead, they told him to go home. Amaziah, who was a big-shot preacher in Israel, said to Amos, "Go home! We don't want to hear what you've got to say. Go back to Judah and preach that mess to them!"

Now therefore hear thou the word of the Lord: Thou sayest, Prophesy not against Israel, and drop not thy word against the house of Isaac.

—Amos 7:16

Have you ever worked around cattle or sheep? There is a certain aroma, a certain smell, that comes from the feed lot. Amos lived his life as a rancher. He smelled bad. He dressed poorly. His fingers were dirty and stained from pinching fruit all day. Amos stood there and said, "I don't care what you say. I'm not going home until God tells me to. I didn't come up here to preach a message to make you feel good. I came up here to bring a word from God. Amen!"

But the people didn't want to hear a word from God. Instead, they wanted to listen to false teachers and preachers like Amaziah. The more things change, the more they stay the same. Today, like in Amos' time, people want to have their ears tickled. Today, false teachers have thrown out the Word of God and replaced it with a bunch of nonsense.

A few years back, one of America's most popular preachers was being interviewed by Larry King. Larry King asked this preacher, "Do you believe that Jesus is the only way to Heaven." He said, "I'd rather not judge. It's not for me to judge." Larry King asked, "Well, what about Muslims? What about Buddhists?" The preacher said, "I'd rather not judge them." Larry King, who is not a believer, was amazed. He asked, "What about an atheist? Are you telling me that you don't want to pass judgment on an atheist? The popular preacher said, "It's not up to me. I don't know a man's heart. I just really can't say."

The Bible says in the last days, the people will heap to themselves teachers, having itching ears. That means they will surround themselves with teachers who will teach them what their itching ears want to hear.

It is not my responsibility to tell you what you want to hear. It is my responsibility to preach the unvarnished truth of the Word of God and let the chips fall where they may. And I don't care what some popular preacher said. Jesus said, "I am not a way." Jesus said, "I am the Way. I am the Truth. I am the Life, and no man comes to the Father except through Me!" That's the Gospel truth!

A Staggering Society

And they shall wander from sea to sea, and from the north even to the east, they shall run to and fro to seek the word of the LORD, and shall not find it.

—Amos 8:12

Amos tells the people that they will wander. The Hebrew word for "wander" means "to stagger like a drunk with no direction to your life." They would become a staggering society. People are fickle. When they have the Word, they don't want it. When they don't have the Word, then they want it.

A man I went to seminary with was one of the best preachers that I ever heard. He preached the gospel with fire and passion. After seminary, he was called to a nice church. However, he is now a substitute teacher. His church told him to leave. They said he was too fiery.

After they fired my friend, that church called a pastor who preached sermons about bluebirds. In one of his messages, he said, "Christians are like little bluebirds, but we don't have to be blue. We can have a little song in our heart because Jesus is so tweet." Now that church is complaining about that guy. They ran off my friend who preached the truth with passion, and now they gripe because their new preacher is boring.

America is filled with cold, lifeless, dead churches that have lost their first love—Jesus Christ. They may have at one time had a man of God in their midst who preached the Word, but they ran him off because they didn't want to hear. So, God sent a famine. If you don't appreciate and accept the Word of God, you may find yourself without it one day. Then you will wish you had it.

What America needs is a word from God. What does God say when kids are being murdered in schools? What does God say when women are being raped and murdered in the streets? What does God say when babies are being murdered and we call it a "choice"? What does God say when husbands and wives run around on each other? What does God say about parents who beat and molest their children? What does God say about so-called "same-sex marriage"? What does God say about all the nasty sin that's in our world today?

What we need today is a word from God. We need the remedy that's in the Word of God. We need to take our Bibles and let God nourish us.

How can we stop the famine? Start listening. Own up to the fact that we need to get right with God. Admit we need to get real and get right with God. God says, "If my people, which are called by my name, shall humble themselves, and pray, and seek my face, and turn from their wicked ways; then will I hear from Heaven, and will forgive their sin, and will heal their land" (2 Chronicles 7:14). We need to do it now before He goes silent.

One of my favorite movies is *The Blind Side*. Sandra Bullock won the 2010 Best Actress Academy Award for her portrayal of Leigh Ann Tuohy in *The Blind Side*. The film tells the story of a Christian family who took in a homeless young man and gave him the chance to reach his God-given potential. Michael Oher not only overcame the hopelessness of his dysfunctional inner-city upbringing but became the first-round NFL draft pick for the Baltimore Ravens in 2009.

A couple of years ago, at a fund-raising dinner, Sean Tuohy said the transformation of his family and Michael all started with two words. One night, when they spotted Michael walking along the road in the coldness of

November wearing shorts and a T-shirt, Leigh Ann Tuohy said two words that changed their world. She told her husband, "Turn around." Turn around. They turned the car around, loaded Michael in their warm vehicle, and ultimately adopted him into their family.

Turn around. Those same two words can change your life. Literally, "turn around" is what the word "repent" means. When you turn around, you change directions. You can turn around and start an exciting new life.

Today, you may need to turn around and believe in Jesus Christ. Or you may need to turn around and rededicate your life to the Lord. Whatever your situation, a great story of wonderful change could be just two words away. Turn around.

It's time to turn around before God sends a famine. Do it before God quits speaking to your heart. Do it before all you hear is the silence of God.

Turn around now.

Did You Know?

In Amos 9:11, God said, "In that day will I raise up the tabernacle of David that is fallen, and close up the breaches thereof; and I will raise up his ruins, and I will build it as in the days of old." This messianic prophecy reveals that God will bring blessing after judgment and will ultimately restore Israel. The reference to the restoration of David's "tabernacle" refers to the reinstatement of David's rule through Jesus the Messiah (see Acts 15:15–17).

A Moment of Prophecy

Amos spoke of a famine of hearing the words of the LORD. This was the most horrific proclamation possible. It was the greatest curse imaginable. Amos predicted a future in which men would stagger from sea to sea, from the Mediterranean to the Persian Gulf, and they will find nothing. They will search for the Word of the Lord, but they will not find it. God told His people in Deuteronomy 8:3 that they could not live on bread alone. They needed the Word of God. Through Amos, God told His people that they will be denied the sustenance of his Word because of their ingratitude and disobedience. For four hundred years, God stopped sharing His written Word with Israel. From the closing of the book of Malachi to the opening of the book of Matthew, there was a great gap of revelatory silence. There was a famine in the land, a famine of the Word of God. With the birth of Jesus, the famine came to an end.

CHAPTER 4

Unchristian Christian

The vision of Obadiah. Thus saith the Lord GOD concerning Edom; We have heard a rumour from the LORD, and an ambassador is sent among the heathen, Arise ye, and let us rise up against her in battle. Behold, I have made thee small among the heathen: thou art greatly despised.

—Obadiah 1-2

The small German town of Herzogenaurach might seem a sleepy backwater place, but it's home to two of the world's top sportswear companies. For decades, the rivalry between two brothers split the town in two. The rivalry was all about shoes.

Rudolf and Adolf Dassler started out making shoes together before having a terrible falling out. Their argument resulted in the creation of two sports giants, Puma and Adidas, both still based in the provincial town.

Rudolf and his younger brother Adolf—Rudi and Adi to friends—began their shoe business in their mother's laundry room in the 1920s. Their new, lightweight sports shoes began to attract attention and they moved into a location south of the Aurach river near the train station.

The Dassler's shoe factory jumped onto the world stage in 1936 when they found themselves providing footwear for American Jessie Owens, who won four gold medals at the Berlin Olympics. However, after the war, their relationship fell apart. Today, no one is certain how their argument started. Some think it could have had something to do with Nazi Party links and that after Rudolf was picked up by American soldiers and accused of being a member of the SS, he was convinced his brother had turned him in. Others speculate it could have had something to do with their wives or a simple misunderstanding in a bomb shelter. No one knows for sure.

What is certain is that they felt they could no longer work together. So, in 1948, the Dassler's shoe factory was split in two. Rudolf Dassler packed his bags and moved to the other side of the river. There he established Puma. From there on in, the town was split in two like a sort of mini-Berlin with the little river as a partition in the middle. Like Berlin's famous wall, people were unable to cross over—at least when it came to shoes.

Two camps formed around loyalty to shoe brands.

There were stores, bakers, and bars which were known as either loyal to Rudolf's Puma, or Adolf's Adidas. There were two soccer teams: the ASV Herzogenaurach Club wore the three stripes; the 1FC Herzogenaurach had the jumping cat on its footwear. Intermarriage was frowned upon.

Ernst Ditrich, who works at the town's museum recalled, "I knew a butcher who played for the Puma team. He told us the guys from the Adidas team didn't need to bother buying at his store. He didn't want to do business with them. That sort of thing happened, and still does."

The brothers never did reconcile. They remained enemies for the rest of their lives.

Obadiah

Obadiah means "serving YAHWEH" in Hebrew, derived from דָּבַע ('avad) meaning "to serve" and הָי (yah) referring to God.

While they are buried in the same cemetery, their graves are about as far apart as possible. Sadly, their family feud still rages in Herzogenaurach. People in the Bavarian town tend to look down to see what kind of shoes you are wearing before they strike up a conversation.

There is nothing quite as brutal and cruel as family rivalry, particularly when hatred arises between brothers. From Cain and Abel to Rudolf and Adolf Dassler, the rivalry between brothers has often resulted in heartache and tragedy. Cain murdered his brother, Abel. The Dassler brothers hated each other and divided a town. Shouldn't these brothers have known better? Cain and Abel, and Rudolf and Adolf Dassler were both raised by godly parents. Yet, they still acted ungodly.

I am often asked if I am surprised by all the unrestrained sin in the world today. I really am not. We shouldn't be surprised when lost people act like lost people. However, I am surprised when people who should know better, when Christians, act like the lost.

Obadiah had a message for people who behaved poorly when they should have known better. Obadiah's message was unusual. Unlike the other prophets, he did not speak to the Northern Nation of Israel or the Southern Nation of Judah. Instead, he preached to the nation of Edom.

The story does not begin in Obadiah, however. For that, we must go back to the book of Genesis. There we read about a conflict between two brothers that started in the womb of their mother Rebekah. The twin boys were fighting in utero, and Rebekah asked the Lord why this was happening. God answered, "Two nations are in thy womb, and two manner of people shall be separated from thy bowels; and the one people shall be stronger than the other people; and the elder shall serve the younger" (Genesis 25:23). These were no ordinary boys, and they would play a huge part in God's plan for the ages. In conflict from birth, Rebekah's twins continued to struggle with each other throughout their lives, and their descendants would continue to the family tradition.

Edom descended from Esau, the son of Isaac and Rebekah and the brother of Jacob (Genesis 25:19≠34). Edom means "red," the color of Esau's hair and the color of the stew for which he sold his birthright.

In Genesis, we read that from Jacob and Esau came two nations. Jacob's name was changed to Israel, and his twelve sons founded the nation of Israel—the chosen nation from which came the Lord Jesus Christ. Jacob's brother, Esau, founded the nation of Edom.

Jacob talked Esau out of his birthright for a plate of stew (Genesis 25:27–34). Later, he tricked his father Isaac into blessing him instead of Esau (Genesis 27). Esau took the lesser inheritance and went down to Mount Seir in Edom. Esau chased the Horites out from Mount Hor and took over this mountainous area of cave dwellings. The word *hor* in Hebrew means "caves" (Genesis 32:3; 33:14–16).

Edom's major towns were Teman in the south, Bozrah in the north, and Sela, the capital city, hidden away in the most inaccessible part of the dark red sandstone highlands. Today, we know Sela as Petra. The city is entered through a mile-long narrow winding gorge or canyon, called a *siq*. Petra is a tourist attraction today and was featured in the film *Indiana Jones and The Last Crusade*.

The descendants of Esau hated the

Exploring the caves of Petra

descendants of Jacob because Esau lost his birthright. This age-old conflict continued to emerge at various times in Israel's history. For example, during Israel's journey to the Promised Land, the king of Edom denied Israel permission to travel through the country of Edom, thus making their trip more difficult (Numbers 20:14-21). The conflict continued to rage after Israel's conquest of Canaan. David conquered Edom for a time (2 Samuel 8:13-14), but the Edomites struck back during the reigns of Jehoshaphat (2 Chronicles 20:1-2) and Joram (2 Kings 8:20-22). Later, under King Amaziah, Judah regained the upper hand and severely punished the Edomites, casting many of them off the top of a cliff (2 Chronicles 25: 11-12).

So, there was a long history of hate between Edom and Israel. But when the Babylonian Empire spread westward, Edom and Israel made a treaty to assist each other. However, Edom refused to help Israel and instead joined with the Babylonians to destroy Jerusalem and the Temple.

The Babylonians gave the Jewish lands to the Edomites to replace the Jews that had been killed and taken into captivity. The Edomites left Petra and occupied the Jewish lands. Around the same time, the Nabateans—descendants of Ishmael through Nebajoth (Genesis 25:13) came up from Arabia and settled in Petra.

The Jews throughout history had trouble with the Edomites in their land after they returned from Babylon. They were called Idumeans or Edumeans by the Romans. When the Romans conquered Israel, they put the Edomites in charge. The Herods were Edomites.

> ### Date
>
> **Edom was allied with the Babylonians at the fall of Jerusalem in 587/586 B.C. Therefore, Obadiah was written in that period.**

At the time Jesus entered the world, who was the king of Judea? It was King Herod. When Jesus, a descendant of Jacob, stood before King Herod, a descendant of Esau, it was another manifestation of the conflict between Rebekah's sons.

So, after A.D. 70, when the Jews were either killed, sold into slavery, or escaped into other nations, the Edomites were left in the land. The so-called "Palestinians" today are really the descendants of Esau. They are Edomites. The Edomites (Palestinians) hate the Jews because they believe the land of Israel belongs to them. Understanding this history helps you to make sense of the constant state of conflict in Israel today.

> **The pride of thine heart hath deceived thee, thou *that dwellest in the clefts of the rock*, whose habitation is high; that saith in his heart, Who shall bring me down to the ground?**
>
> —Obadiah 3

So, Obadiah preached to the Edomites who lived in Petra. He declared God would judge the Edomites. God would destroy the Edomites because when the Babylonians came and destroyed Jerusalem, they just stood by and watched. Remember, the Edomites were descended from Abraham. They were part of the family. The Edomites and the Israelites were both members of the family of God. Yet, the Edomites acted like they were outside of the family of God.

As Christians, this is a message we need to hear. Christians should act like Christians. The Bible says we should act like Jesus. If we could ever get people on the inside of our churches acting like Jesus, we would have no problem reaching the lost outside the church. Sadly, today most Christians don't act very Christlike. Instead, they act like unchristian Christians.

Obadiah teaches us three things about the behavior of the Edomites that we can apply to our Christian life today. There are three lessons we can learn from Obadiah about how not to act.

Contemplation

In the day that thou *stoodest on the other side*, in the day that the strangers carried away captive his forces, and foreigners entered into his gates,

and cast lots upon Jerusalem, even thou wast as one of them. But *thou shouldest not have looked* **on the day of thy brother. ...**

—Obadiah 11–12a

The Edomites contemplated. They stood and watched as their brothers were in trouble, but they didn't help. They stood and watched as their brothers were taken captive.

Obadiah said to the Edomites that they acted like lost people. They behaved like heathens or pagans. They didn't help when the Babylonians invaded Israel. They never lifted a finger. They said, "It's not my fight. I'm not getting involved. We are not our brother's keeper."

However, God says that you are your brother's keeper. You have a responsibility to other people in the family of God. You should not sit idly by while the world goes to hell and God's people suffer.

There are people like the Edomites in the church today. They never lift a finger. They never work in the nursery, teach a Sunday school class, serve as a greeter, or even financially give. They just sit and take up space. In the church today, three percent of the people carry eighty percent of the load. The rest are like hobos on a train—they did not pay for a ticket. They are just along for the ride.

Jesus said, "Even as the Son of man came not to be ministered unto, but to minister, and to give his life a ransom for many" (Matthew 20:28). In other words, Jesus said that He came to serve. However, there are unchris-

> ### *Did You Know?*
>
> In Bible times, Petra was designated as one of the cities of refuge where an unjustly persecuted person could go to find food and shelter. David went to Petra to find safety from the attempts of Saul to kill him. The Apostle Paul went to Petra, which was at that time was part of Northern Arabia. Paul stayed there for three years to escape the Jews who wanted to kill him (Galatians 1:17).

tian Christians who won't use Christ's example and act as servants. How can you say that you are a follower of the servant Savior and just sit there every week and do nothing for the family of God?

The Lord Jesus Christ left His home in Heaven and came to this world where He lived a sinless life. Then, one day, He was crucified. He gave His blood to pay for your sins. He died and was buried. But three days later, Jesus rose from the dead. He did all of that so you might have life, life more abundantly, and eternal life. Jesus gave His life for you. Grace and gratitude should make you want to serve Him.

Besides, it's a privilege to serve the Lord. It's a privilege to visit a sick person in the hospital. It's a privilege to pray for someone. It's a privilege to give. It's a privilege to encourage people. It's a privilege to teach. It's a privilege to be the hands and feet of Jesus. We can't just act like a lost person and stand and gaze while our brothers and sisters are in need.

In 1956, a twelve-year-old, dark-skinned boy walked into a Sunday school class at First Baptist Church in San Antonio, Texas. The little boy didn't talk much. He just quietly sat there. For some reason, nobody talked to him either. It could have been because he looked different. It could have been because he wasn't originally from America. It could have been because he was quiet. Whatever the reason, nobody in that great big church ever talked to that twelve-year-old boy.

The little boy sat in a Sunday school class for three years. He sat there for three years, and nobody ever talked to that young man. Then, one day, he was gone. He left and never came back to that church.

Nine years later, one of his Sunday school teachers recognized that young man. That dark-skinned young man from Jordan was on the news. The Sunday school teacher began to shed tears as she realized that she had been given an opportunity to impact his life, but she missed it. She had just sat and looked at that young man who was in her class for those three years. Sadly, in all that time, she never once told him about Jesus.

The young man who sat in that Sunday school class for three years was named Sirhan Sirhan. When he was twenty-four years old, Sirhan Sirhan shot and killed Senator Robert Kennedy. Would history be different if someone would have shared the saving Gospel of the Lord Jesus Christ with that young man? Sadly, we will never know.

Celebration

But thou shouldest not have looked on the day of thy brother in the day that he became a stranger; neither shouldest thou have *rejoiced* over the children of Judah in the day of their destruction; neither shouldest thou have spoken proudly in the day of distress.

—Obadiah 12

The Edomites contemplated and they also celebrated. The psalmist records the celebration of Edomites, "Remember, O LORD, the children of Edom in the day of Jerusalem; who said, Rase it, rase it, even to the foundation thereof" (Psalm 137:7). The Edomites cheered on the Babylonian destruction of Jerusalem with shouts of, "Tear it down to its foundations!"

Obadiah says the Edomites "rejoiced." Defeat in any form is difficult enough in itself to endure, but the sting of defeat is made worse when someone else rejoices over your defeat. Not only did the Edomites stand idly by and watch as the Babylonians tore down the walls, set fire to the cities, raped the women, murdered, and carried off all the treasures; but they also rejoiced in the misery of their brothers.

Once again, there are people like that in the church today. They never lift a finger to help in the church, but they know about every problem that's going on in the church.

> **Did You Know?**
>
> **Obadiah is the shortest book in the Old Testament. It is only a mere twenty-one verses long.**

And they will run their mouth to anyone who will listen.

I read about this woman named Joan who was the church gossip. Joan went to church with a couple named Lucy and George. One day, Joan saw George's pickup truck parked outside the town's only bar. Joan smiled with happiness and thought to herself, "I knew there was something about that man."

Joan wasted no time. She called all the people at church and told them about George. She said, "You know, Lucy married a drunk." She said, "George is such a sinner." She said, "I know for a fact George is an alcoholic because I saw his truck parked at the bar."

When Lucy heard of what was being said behind her back, she was very upset. She told her husband what Joan was telling everyone. She told him Joan saw his truck was parked outside the bar and she said he must be an alcoholic. George stared at her for a moment and didn't say anything. Then he got up, walked out, got in his pickup, drove across town, parked in front of Joan's house, and just left his truck there all night.

Now that's a story with a funny ending. However, it's not funny if someone is celebrating your problems and your misery. As a Christian, you should never celebrate the misfortune of another person. If I ever hear of someone whose kid is in trouble for drugs, or sex, or whatever, I won't celebrate. If I ever hear of someone who is having marital problems, I won't celebrate. If I ever hear of someone having financial problems, I won't celebrate. If I ever hear of someone caught up in sin, I won't celebrate. I won't celebrate, gossip, or criticize because but for the grace of God, that could be me going through that trial.

Cooperation

Neither shouldest thou have stood in the crossway, to cut off those of his that did escape; neither shouldest thou have delivered up those of his that did remain in the day of distress.

—Obadiah 14

This is what the Edomites did to their family. The Edomites contemplated, celebrated, and they also cooperated. They aided the enemy. As the Jewish men and women fled from their invaders, their brothers, the Edomites, stood at the crossroads waiting for them and either killed, captured, or returned them to their enemies. This was the worst treachery that could be imagined, one brother murdering another, or sending a brother back into a dangerous situation that might very well lead to his death.

Today, many Christians are cooperating with the enemy. Christians are actually cooperating with Satan. How so, you ask? What about people who say they are Christians, but they haven't done a Christian thing in years? Lost people look at Christians like that and say, "If that's what being a Christian is all about, then I don't want any part of it." What about people like that?

What about people who come every week to the church of the Living God and sit there like these Edomites, looking like they had a big ole glass of pickle juice for breakfast. They never smile. All they do is frown. Then, whenever somebody in the church has a new idea, they say, "We've never done it that way before!" What about people like that?

What about people who come to church every Sunday, but they live like hell all week long. You can't tell the difference between the way they behave and the way a lost person behaves. What about people like that?

What about the Christian who "goes along to get along"? They don't want to offend anyone, so they never speak out on the social issues of our day. They never take a stand for Christian morals and values. What about people like that?

Several years ago, a father in Connecticut took his newborn child out of the delivery room and violently threw the baby onto the floor. Due to the force of the fall, the infant's skull ruptured, and fragments of brain were left oozing on the floor. Christians in the community were outraged and demanded justice, as well they should. Eventually, the father was arrested and charged with first-degree murder.

Ironically, however, just one hour before, in the same hospital where the father murdered his child, a medical doctor suctioned a living fetus from a mother's womb only to cut off its head; and he was paid thousands of dollars to do it. Not one Christian spoke up for that child. The tragedy is that the United States is the most Christianized nation in the world. We know who God is. We know what God expects. However, we sit idly by, not wanting to stand up or speak up.

Most of what is wrong with this country is due to apostasy in the pulpit, and apathy in the pew. America's greatest problem is not political, but spiritual. Much of the fault rests on the shoulders of God's people, the church of the Lord Jesus Christ.

Rather than having more of the church in the world, there is more world in the church; thus, making it difficult to tell the two apart. We are becoming more and more pagan every single day. It is not pagan America that needs revival. It is not the baby-killing abortionist that needs revival. It is not the liquor-selling bartender that needs revival. It is not the wild living prostitute that needs revival. No. It is the lazy, lifeless, lukewarm church

> ### *Did You Know?*
>
> **Obadiah 17 describes a day when "the house of Jacob" shall possess her possessions and reclaim her land. This prophecy was partially fulfilled in 1948. However, the next four verses describe the complete control of the land and the kingdom being the Lord's, which will happen in the Millennium.**

that needs revival. But instead of seeking God and holiness, we are acting no different than those who are lost.

The world is going to Hell. The world is as lost as a snake; like a dog in high weeds; like a goose in a snowstorm; and the greatest holdback to reaching the lost are God's people. We act like unchristian Christians.

In the day that thou stoodest on the other side, in the day that the

strangers carried away captive his forces, and foreigners entered into his gates, and cast lots upon Jerusalem, *even thou wast as one of them.*

—Obadiah 11

What would Obadiah say to unchristian Christians? We find the answer in the last line of Obadiah 11 which reads, "… even thou wast as one of them." In other words, you're acting like a lost person. Obadiah said, "You're acting like one of them."

Obadiah's message is timeless. Do you remember the story of Noah? Noah preached a gospel message. He built an ark with one door. The only way to get saved was to go into the ark through the one door. Noah's ark was a picture of Jesus. Noah preached a gospel message. But after the flood, Noah got drunk, and Noah got naked. I can just see Obadiah telling Noah, "You're acting like one of them."

Remember Abraham? Abraham had a beautiful wife. She was so beautiful, he was worried she would be taken from him. So, he lied and said she was his sister. I can just see Obadiah saying to Abraham, "You're acting like one of them."

Remember David? When he should have been off to war, he was at home committing adultery with Bathsheba. I can just see Obadiah saying to David, "You're acting like one of them."

Remember Solomon? Solomon had more godly wisdom than any man who ever lived. But he was taken in by the idolatry of his many wives. I can just see Obadiah saying to Solomon, "You're acting like one of them."

Remember Simon Peter? Peter denied the Lord Jesus three times. He even cursed for emphasis. I can see Obadiah saying to Peter, "You're acting like one of them."

Remember those today who profess the name of Jesus Christ, but sin just like the rest of the world. Obadiah would say, "You're acting like one of them. You're acting like an unchristian Christian."

A Christian is a mind through which Jesus thinks. A Christian is a heart through which Jesus lives. A Christian is a voice through which Jesus speaks. A Christian is a hand through which Jesus helps. Are you acting like a Christian, or are you acting like one of them? Are you acting like an unchristian Christian?

Compassion

And saviours shall come up on mount Zion to judge the mount of Esau; and the kingdom shall be the LORD's.

—Obadiah 21

Despite the Edomites' contemplation, celebration, and cooperation; God showed compassion. Obadiah spoke of God's compassion in verse 21 when he used the word, "saviours." "Saviours," or our modern English word "saviors," means "those who have been rescued." God showed compassion by extending grace—grace for Israel. Someday Israel will rule the Edomite kingdom again.

God also extended grace for the Edomites. God promised that those who repent and turn to Him will be saved. He who calls on the name of the Lord shall be saved. That is grace. Grace is something you don't deserve, but God gives it to you anyway.

I was a lost sinner. I deserved death and Hell. But one day, I found Jesus, and He saved my soul. The Lord Jesus Christ gave me grace. I didn't deserve it, but He took my place. Jesus was beaten, tortured, and nailed to a cross. He died a miserable death. He did that for me.

He did it for you too. All you need to do is to accept His sacrifice. All you need to do is accept His grace.

In his book *The Preaching Event*, John Claypool tells a story about identical twin brothers who never married because they enjoyed each other's company so much. When their father died, they took over his store and ran it together in a joyful collaboration.

One day a man came into the brother's store to make a small purchase and paid for it with a dollar. The brother who made the sale placed the dollar on top of the cash register. Then he walked the customer to the door to say goodbye. When he returned, the dollar bill was gone.

He asked his twin brother, "Did you take the dollar bill I left here?"

"No, I didn't," answered the brother.

"Surely, you took it," he said, "There was nobody else in the store."

The brother became angry: "I'm telling you; I did not take the dollar bill."

From that point, mistrust and suspicion grew until finally, the two brothers could not work together. They put a partition right down the middle of the building and made it into two stores. In anger, they refused to speak for the next twenty years.

One day a stranger pulled up in a car and entered one of the two stores. "Have you been in business very long here?" the stranger asked.

"Yes, thirty or forty years," was the answer.

"Good," continued the stranger, "I very much need to tell you Something … Some twenty years ago, I passed through this town. I was out of work and homeless. I jumped off a boxcar. I had no money and I had not eaten for days. I came down that alley outside and when I looked in your store window, I saw a dollar bill on the cash register. I slipped in and took it. Recently I became a Christian. I was converted and accepted Christ as my personal Savior. I know now it was wrong of me to steal that dollar bill … and I have come to pay you back with interest and to beg your forgiveness."

When the stranger finished his confession, the old storekeeper began to weep as he said, "Would you do me a favor? Would you please come next door and tell that story to my brother?" Of course, with the second telling, the two brothers were reconciled with many hugs, apologies, and tears.

Twenty years of hurt and broken relationship based not on fact, but on mistrust and misunderstanding. But then healing came; reconciliation came, because of that stranger's love for Christ.

Is there someone in your life with whom you need to be reconciled? If you are a Christian, Jesus on the cross extended grace to you. Shouldn't you extend grace too?

If you are not a Christian, let me remind you that God is a God of grace, mercy, and forgiveness. God is a God of second chances. Even if you have stumbled; even if you have fallen; Jesus is here today, and He is offering grace. He is waiting to reach out his nail-scarred hand and pull you back up.

Won't you reach out to Him?

A Moment of Prophecy

Petra will be Israel's hiding place for the last half of the Tribulation (Psalm 60:1, 9–12; Isaiah 16:1–5). In the middle of the Tribulation, the Antichrist will break his covenant with Israel and exalt himself as God (2 Thessalonians 2:4). The Jews will have to flee quickly for their lives (Matthew 24:16–31). They will flee to Petra, where the Lord will take care of them for 1,260 days, the last three and a half years of the Tribulation (Revelation 12:6).

CHAPTER 5

The Fugitive

Now the word of the LORD came unto Jonah the son of
Amittai, saying, Arise, go to Nineveh, that great city, and
cry against it; for their wickedness is come up before me.
But Jonah rose up to flee unto Tarshish from the presence of the LORD, and went down to Joppa; and he found
a ship going to Tarshish: so he paid the fare thereof, and
went down into it, to go with them unto Tarshish from
the presence of the LORD.

—Jonah 1:1–3

Once there was a man named Henry, who was an avid hunter. He loved hunting, and his life-long dream was to go to Africa for a safari. He used to watch
TV shows about men on safari, and he would dream about hunting big game
on the African plains. So, Henry saved up for years until he had enough for his
dream safari in Africa.

The day finally arrived, and when Henry got to Africa, he hired a tour
guide to lead the safari. The tour guide took him out to one of the best places
to hunt. They had just arrived when suddenly a huge man-eating lion jumped
out and ran straight for them. They both took off running and screaming as the
lion chased after them. As they were running, the tour guide stopped, and sat

down on a rock and started untying his hiking boots. He reached into his back-pack and pulled out a pair of Nike running shoes and he started to lace them up. Henry ran past him and said, "Man are you crazy? You know that you can't outrun a lion in tennis shoes." The tour guide said, "I'm not trying to outrun the lion. I just have to outrun you."

Here's the truth: I don't know if it is possible to outrun a lion, but I do know it is impossible to outrun the Lion of Judah. You can't outrun the Lord, but it is amazing how many people try.

Jonah

From the Hebrew name יֹנָה **(Yonah)** mean-ing "dove."

Your life is a race. You might be on the right track. You might be on the wrong track. You might be on the good path. You might be on the bad path. You might be running for God. You might be running from God. You might even be a *Christian* running from God—a fugitive Christian.

There was an old TV program called "The Fugitive." It was also made into a movie starring Harrison Ford several years ago. In the television show and the movie, Dr. Richard Kimball was falsely accused of killing his wife, and he was on the run. "The Fugitive" was about a man on the run, and there are many Christians today who are running from God. They are fugitive Christians. That is exactly what Jonah was in the New Testament sense of the term.

Jonah was an unusual prophet, and he had an unusual story. He is by far the most well-known of the twelve Minor Prophets. His story of being swallowed by a big fish has been enjoyed by children for generations. When our kids were little, we used to read to them from a children's book version of Jonah. When I was little, my mom used to read the same children's book to me.

We know Jonah was a prophet of God long before we find this message coming to him in the book of Jonah. He first showed up in 2 Kings where he prophesied the Lord would expand the borders of Israel (2 Kings 14:21–25). So, Jonah was a man who prophesied to the people of Israel. However, in the book that bears his name, the Lord called Jonah to go to Nineveh.

Nineveh was the capital of the Assyrian Empire. It was in what is now northern Iraq—a suburb of the modern city of Mosul. The Assyrians themselves had a well-deserved reputation for utter ruthlessness and barbarity toward any who stood against them. They would often skin alive the people they conquered. The Assyrians were the bitter enemies of the Jews. A state of hostilities existed between the two peoples, and the Assyrians eventually conquered and took into captivity the Northern Kingdom of Israel in 722–721 B.C.

The city of Nineveh was massive. It was about seven miles in circumference, with stone walls and towers over two hundred feet high and fifty feet thick—wide enough for six chariots abreast. The city was famous for its walls, and for its gates which were named after Assyrian gods. Nineveh was also famous for the worship of Ishtar (Astarte), the fertility goddess. It was a city that was full of temples (around two thousand) to many different deities including Sin, Nergal, Shamash, and Nabu, just to name a few.

Today Nineveh is in ruins, but parts of the walls and the gates still stand. During my military career, I was deployed to Iraq, and I spent time in Mosul. I preached the saving Gospel of the Lord Jesus Christ at the gates of Nineveh, so I feel sort of kinship with Jonah because I have stood where Jonah stood, and I have preached where Jonah preached. Also, like Jonah, there have been times in my life when I have been a fugitive from God.

Praying with U.S. Army soldiers at the gates of Nineveh (Mosul, Iraq).

God told Jonah to go to a place where they butchered their enemies, practiced idolatry, offered human sacrifices, and worshiped through temple prostitutes. In the eyes of a man of God such as Jonah, the Assyrians were an abomination worthy of the full measure of a righteous God's wrath.

Imagine for a moment if you as a Christian, had a neighbor who worshiped the devil, beat you up whenever you walked past, and raped your daughters. Then imagine that the Lord says to you that He is going to judge your neighbor for his wickedness … and He wants you to take the news to your neighbor! What would you do?

> **But Jonah rose up to flee unto Tarshish from the presence of the LORD, and went down to Joppa; and he found a ship going to Tarshish: so he paid the fare thereof, and went down into it, to go with them unto Tarshish from the presence of the LORD.**
>
> —Jonah 1:3

The Bible says Jonah ran; he rose to "flee" to Tarshish. The word *flee* means "to run away from." It comes from a Hebrew word that means to be a fugitive. Jonah was a fugitive.

Stop and think about that for a moment. Jonah was a man of God—a child of God—a man who loved God—a man who worshipped God—but he was a fugitive from God. Today, you can sit in church every Sunday and be a fugitive because you are running from God. You can be a Bible-toting, Scripture-quoting, blood-bought believer, and still be running from God. You can profess the name of Jesus and be a fugitive Christian.

> **Date**
>
> Jonah was a prophet in the time when Jeroboam II was king of Israel. This places the book sometime between 780 and 750 B.C.

Being a fugitive Christian has nothing to do with your salvation. It has nothing to do with going to Heaven. The devil can't take your salvation. Being a fugitive Christian has nothing to do with your *destination*; it has everything to do with your *destiny*.

A Disobedient Path

There are three dangers you face if you are a fugitive Christian. There are three dangers you face if you run from God, and they progressively get worse. First, if you run from God, you are following a disobedient path.

Now the word of the LORD came unto Jonah the son of Amittai, saying,

—Jonah 1:1

The Bible says the "word of the Lord" came to Jonah. The phrase "the word of the Lord" means the command of God. When God speaks, disobedience is not an option. The Bible says the command of the Lord came to Jonah. The command of God, the Father, came to Jonah.

I was raised by parents who spoiled me rotten. Consequently, I was a little ornery as a boy. So, I got more whippings than all the other kids in our family combined. I understand that spanking children is not politically correct in this modern, sophisticated society, but I was raised in a different time by a different generation of people. My parents believed when children misbehaved, it was okay to spank them. Since I misbehaved often, I was spanked regularly. I was never abused, but when I acted up, my backside was busted.

Because I was always in trouble, I had a favorite place that I used to hide. I built a fort in the woods behind our house. It was made from some logs that were covered with pine branches. The pine branches were perfect cam-

> **Did You Know?**
>
> Through the entire book of Jonah, the prophet refers to himself in the third person.

ouflage. When I was in my fort, I could not be seen. I was completely hidden.

One day, when I was about nine or ten years old, I was playing outside with my cousin. His name was Jimmy Joe Jeff Johnny Paul Ray Elmer Junior, but that was a mouthful. So, we just called him Bubba. Anyway, I was in the yard with Bubba. To this day, I don't remember how we started arguing. I just remember he made me mad. He said something that agitated me, and he was just standing there with his jaw sticking out. So, I balled up my fist like I was going to hit him. I knew the consequences of hitting my cousin, and I really did not mean to hit him. All I was going to do was let the wind brush him in the face to scare him, but I caught the end of his chin and lifted him off the ground. Bubba fell backward on his behind. Then he jumped right back up and screamed, "I'm telling your dad on you!"

I ran to the woods to my fort where I was totally hidden. Nobody could find me. Through the pine needles, I saw dad step out the back door with a belt. He kept two belts. One was for holding up his pants, and the other he hung on a nail on the wall under a copy of that old hymn, "I Need Thee Every Hour." That was the belt he used on me.

> **Did You Know?**
>
> **Nineveh was founded by Nimrod—the first world dictator (Genesis 10:9–12).**

Dad stood at the back door, and he yelled, "James, come here. I see you out there in the woods." I was stunned because I was completely hidden. How could he see me? Surely, he must have X-ray vision like Superman. He yelled again, "Boy, I see you between those logs with those branches over you there in the woods. Come here now."

I stepped out and started shuffling toward him. Dad loudly and sternly said, "You had better run." So, I started running. As I was running, I thought, "James, you are dumb. Who in their right mind would run toward a spanking?" So, I pivoted and started running in the other direction. To my amazement, my old man started chasing me.

In my mind, I thought I could outrun him. I was younger and faster. However, as I was running, I thought, "James, you sure are dumb. You can't live in the woods. You've got to come home sooner or later to eat." So, I just slid down. It was a bad day after that.

A Drawn-Out Path

It hurt me when I ran from my father, but it really hurts you when you run from your Heavenly Father. When you run from God, you are on a disobedient path. It is a disobedient path because it is a drawn-out path. You end up taking the long way.

Arise, go to Nineveh, that great city, and cry against it; for their wickedness is come up before me.

—Jonah 1:2

God told Jonah to "arise." In other words, God told Jonah to "get up." God didn't say, "I want to run something by you and see what you think." God didn't say, "If it is convenient with you." God didn't say, "Would you pray about it?" God said, "Get up." When God says, "Get up," you had better get up.

There is a built-in Garmin Navigator—a GPS—in the dashboard of my truck. It is an incredible piece of technology. All I do is type in an address. Then a voice starts talking that tells me where to go. It's a woman's voice. I named the voice Betty. She is Betty Ford …

Whenever I miss a turn, Betty gets mad. She seems to have a huff in her voice, "Huff, Recalculating. Recalculating route." Then she will tell me an alternative route. The route will always take me back to the original road, but it will be the long way around.

God has one road for your life. If you choose not to follow that road, then you are on the wrong road. God has a road for your life, and it is easy to take the long route. The journey away from God begins with a single disobedient step. It is that easy to become a fugitive Christian.

A Defective Path

But Jonah rose up to flee unto Tarshish from the presence of the Lord,

and went down to Joppa; and he found a ship going to Tarshish: so he paid the fare thereof, and went down into it, to go with them unto Tarshish from the presence of the LORD.

—Jonah 1:3

Not only is the disobedient path a drawn-out path, but it is also a defective path. God told Jonah to go to Nineveh, but he went in the opposite direction. Nineveh is due east; Tarshish is due west. Jonah went in the opposite direction—out of the will of God—on a defective path. God told Jonah to go, but Jonah said to God, "I'm not going where you want me to go. I'm going where I want to go."

In his mind, Jonah believed he could run from God. That is ridiculous! God is everywhere. If you run to get away from God, you're just running from God to God!

Jonah's Journey

If God puts you on a path, He will give you what you need to stay on that path. If God calls you to do something, then step out. God is everywhere, so He is one step ahead of you. Whatever God tells you to do; He will give you the power to do it. Don't make the mistake of getting on a defective path.

Is God calling you to tell a friend about Jesus? Tell that friend. Is God calling you to teach a Sunday school class? Teach that class. Is God calling you to sing special music? Sing those songs. Is God calling you to come back to Him? Come back to God now. Is God calling you to get saved? Give your life to Christ today. God is calling you. Quit running.

A Downward Place

But Jonah rose up to flee unto Tarshish from the presence of the LORD, and went *down* to Joppa; and he found a ship going to Tarshish: so he paid the fare thereof, and went *down* into it, to go with them unto Tarshish from the presence of the LORD.

—Jonah 1:3

Not only was Jonah on a disobedient path, but that path took him to a downward place. Jonah went down to Joppa. He went down into a ship. Eventually, he ended up down in the ocean and down in the belly of a fish. The reason some people are so miserable is because they are running from God, and life is just down.

Over the years, I have known many Christians that are up and down. One week they are up, but the next week they are down. One week they come to church, but the next week they don't come to church. One week they are praising God, but the next week you couldn't find them with a search warrant. One week they are on fire for Jesus, but the next week they are cold and dead inside.

A few years ago, I was traveling on business and stopped to spend the night in a hotel. There were only two floors in that hotel—only two floors—and my room was on the second floor. So, I stepped into the elevator and the doors closed behind me. I pushed the "2" button, and the elevator went up. When the elevator reached the second floor, the doors didn't open, and it went back down. Before I could push another button, the elevator went up again. Once again, the doors didn't open, and the elevator went back down.

That happened five or six times. The elevator went up and down, up and down, but the doors never opened. I started to panic. It dawned on me that I was trapped in an elevator. I reached in my pocket for my cell phone only to discover there was no cellular service in the elevator.

Two or three minutes went by, the entire time I went up and down … up and down … up and down. There was an alarm button on the panel. I pushed the button. On the second floor, there were vending machines right outside the elevator. When I rang the alarm, I heard someone by the vending machines scream, "You kids need to quit playing in the elevator!"

I remembered reading about people who were trapped in an elevator for days. Fear caused me to panic. I began to yell, "Help! I'm trapped on the elevator!" The alarm bell rang, I screamed, and the whole time the elevator went up and down … up and down … up and down.

Suddenly, the elevator jerked and stopped. The doors opened. A man wearing a tool belt was standing there. He said, "Sir, I am sorry, but this elevator is broken. Would you like to take our other elevator?" I said, "No thank you. I'll just take the stairs."

You see, I was tired of going up and down. Don't you get tired of going up and down? Don't you get tired of being hot and cold? Wouldn't you like to move forward this year in your Christian life?

Jonah Lost His Ears

Sadly, Jonah was never up. He was just down. When you go down in life, you lose stuff. First, you lose your ears—your spiritual ears.

> **But the LORD *sent* out a great wind into the sea, and there was a mighty tempest in the sea, so that the ship was like to be broken.**
>
> —Jonah 1:4

The Bible says God "sent" a storm. *Sent* in the Hebrew language means "hurled."

It was like a baseball player throwing a ball. God literally threw a storm at Jonah. Some storms are God-appointed. God was still speaking to Jonah. He was not speaking through His speech; He was speaking through His storm. All of creation was obeying the Creator, but a backslidden prophet could not hear God. It is possible to get so far from God that you don't hear Him anymore.

You can come to church and listen to sermons every Sunday and not hear God. You can lift your hands while singing His songs and not hear God. You can wear a T-shirt that says, "I love Jesus" and not hear God.

How can you hear God today? You have a settled Word from God in the Bible. Read the Bible. What does the Bible say? It doesn't matter what society says—the Bible says it is wrong to live in sin. It doesn't matter what the Supreme Court says—the Bible says it is wrong to murder babies in their mother's womb. It doesn't matter what the government says—the Bible says it is wrong for a same-sex couple to get married. It doesn't matter what Target says—the Bible says it is wrong for some perverted man dressed like a woman to go in the same bathroom as my wife and little girl. It doesn't matter what our confused culture says—the Bible says there are not many ways to God. The only way is through the shed blood of the Lord Jesus Christ.

Jonah Lost His Energy

Then the mariners were afraid, and cried every man unto his god, and cast forth the wares that were in the ship into the sea, to lighten it of them. But Jonah was gone down into the sides of the ship; and he lay, and was *fast asleep*.

—Jonah 1:5

Not only did Jonah lose his ears, but he also lost his energy. The Bible says he was down in the ship sleeping. The ship was about to sink. The crew was about to drown, so they threw stuff off the boat, But Jonah was asleep. Jonah was so far away from God that he was sleeping in the bottom of the ship.

One of the greatest dangers to our Christian faith today is "Ho Hum" Christianity. Big deal. Who cares? If I don't share the gospel, somebody else will. We have a halfhearted church in a hell-bent world.

Jonah Lost His Effectiveness

And he said unto them, I am an Hebrew; and I fear the LORD, the God of heaven, which hath made the sea and the dry land. Then were the men exceedingly afraid, and said unto him. Why hast thou done this? For the men knew that he fled from the presence of the LORD, because he had told them.

—Jonah 1:9–10

> ### Did You Know?
>
> In Jonah 1:5, the mariners cried out to their own pagan "gods." By Jonah 1:16, the mariners cried out to the one true God. God used Jonah's sin for His glory. The mariners got saved. Grace got the last word.

Jonah lost his ears, his energy, and he lost his effectiveness. Jonah told the pagan crew that he was running from God. They knew he was a man of God who was out of God's will. If you lose your reputation, it is very difficult to get it back. The loss of your reputation—your testimony—can damn souls to Hell. You can cause Christians to go astray. You can ruin relationships. You can destroy churches.

Jonah started to lose his effectiveness early in the story. Jonah 1:3 says that Jonah, "… found a ship going to Tarshish: so he paid the fare thereof." How much money do you think it cost Jonah to buy the ticket to get on the boat? The Bible doesn't tell us. I don't know how much money it cost, but whatever the amount, it cost him more than money.

What was the cost when you took that first drink? What was the cost when you smoked that first joint? What was the cost when you went to bed with that person? What was the cost when you told that lie? What was the cost when you first looked at pornography? What was the cost when you ended that relationship? What was the cost to live in sin? Whatever the cost, it cost Jesus more than that to pay the price to forgive you for those sins.

A Divine Punishment

Now the LORD had prepared a great fish to swallow up Jonah. And Jonah was in the belly of the fish three days and three nights.

—Jonah 1:17

When you are a fugitive Christian, you are following a disobedient path that will take you to a downward place which will lead you to divine punishment. The Lord prepared a great fish to swallow Jonah. God has got him now. He found himself in the belly of a big fish. The Bible called it a "great fish." About eight hundred years later, Jesus called it something different. In Matthew 12:40, Jesus called it a whale. It's amazing to me that people will argue over if it was a fish or a whale. The Hebrew word for "fish" in Jonah is *dahg*, which means a "large sea creature." The Greek word for "whale" that Jesus uses is *ketos*, which also means a "large sea creature." God did not classify animals thousands of years ago according to our modern zoological classification system. As far back as creation, God divided animals into very basic groups. To argue that the Bible is wrong because fish and whales are different animals is ridiculous. A "large sea creature" swallowed Jonah.

> ### Did You Know?
>
> In Matthew 12 and Luke 11, Jesus compares Himself to Jonah. This is the only comparison the Lord Jesus Christ makes of Himself to any prophet. Jesus validates the authenticity of Jonah.

It is also amazing that people say, "A man could not live in the belly of a fish for three days and nights." He can if God made the fish. The Bible says God "prepared" the fish. It was a perfectly suitable environment to sustain Jonah. It was also a perfect place for Jonah to think about his disobedience.

Then Jonah prayed unto the LORD his God out of the fish's belly.

—Jonah 2:1

Did You Know?

The Apostle Paul defined the gospel. He wrote, "For I delivered unto you first of all that which I also received, how that Christ died for our sins according to the scriptures; And that he was buried, and that he rose again the third day according to the scriptures" (1 Corinthians 15:3–4). When Paul says "according to the scriptures" he is speaking of the Old Testament, specifically the book of Jonah. Jonah actually died in the belly of the fish and three days later, God raised him from the dead (see also Matthew 12:39–41; Luke 11:29–32).

God had Jonah in the belly of a fish. Can you imagine what it was like? I imagine it was dark, slimy, and stinky. Can you imagine the smell?

In the belly of the fish, Jonah cried out to God and said, "Lord, I'm asking for mercy. God save me!" In other words, he said, "God I've learned my lesson. Wherever you lead, I'll go!"

When I was a little boy, the movie *Jaws* was released. My parents would not let me watch *Jaws*. But, one day, I was over at my friend Willie's house. Willie's parents had a VCR. While his parents were out of the house, Willie and I watched *Jaws*.

There was a scene in *Jaws* where a man threw fish blood and guts in the water. Suddenly, the shark came up out of the water. Today, with all the great special effects and technology in movies, everybody thinks the shark in *Jaws* looks fake. But back when I was a kid, it didn't look fake. When the shark popped up out of the water, I screamed at the top of my lungs. I had nightmares for a month.

Jaws is a movie—it's nothing but fiction. But this is the truth: The Bible says that a big fish swallowed Jonah. In the fish's belly, Jonah prayed and got right with God. Then the fish spit him up on the shore and Jonah went to Nineveh and did what God wanted him to do in the first place. But he had to go through the ordeal of being swallowed by a fish.

You cannot run from God without God bringing discipline into your life. If you live like hell itself and there is no discipline in your life, that's a pretty good indication you have never been saved.

In the book of Hebrews, the Bible says those God loves, He disciplines. The Bible goes on to say that there are four ways you can respond to the Lord's discipline. You can *refuse* it, and that will bring more discipline. You can *reject* it, and discipline will fall more severely. You can *repent* and come back to God. Or you can *rebel* and say no, and God will take your life. The Bible says there is a sin unto death. If you continue to stay stiff-necked; if you continue to stay away from God, then God will take you out of this world.

> ### *Did You Know?*
>
> **The book of Jonah is read every year, in its original Hebrew and its entirety on Yom Kippur, the Jewish Day of Atonement. This attests to Jonah being a story of grace and mercy offered to sinners.**

Or you will have no reward. You won't lose your salvation. But you will stand before Christ at the judgment and lose your reward. It is a serious thing to toy with a Holy God.

> **And the word of the Lord came unto Jonah *the second time*, saying, Arise, go unto Nineveh, that great city, and preach unto it the preaching that I bid thee.**
>
> —Jonah 3:1-2

The Book of Jonah began, "Now the word of the LORD came unto Jonah. ..." Chapter 3 begins, "And the word of the LORD came unto Jonah the second time. ..." Do you see the similarity? Do you see the difference? Thank God for the difference. Thank God for that second time.

I am especially thankful for the second time, or the one hundred and second time. I am thankful for God's grace. He has every right to exclude us and never use us again once we blow it. But He is the God of the second chance ... and the one hundred and second chance.

The crew of the boat received a second chance. They made vows to the one true God. They got saved (Jonah 1:16). The people of Nineveh received a second chance. The entire city—including the king—repented and got saved (Jonah 3:10). And Jonah received a second chance. God was determined to do the work through Jonah, so He did not give up on the reluctant prophet. He gave him a second chance. One of the greatest lessons from the Book of Jonah is God is the God of the second chance even for fugitive Christians.

Many years ago, a man named Fred stood at a crossroads in life. Several years earlier when Fred was a teenager, he had gone to church camp. There, God called him to the ministry.

As Fred became a man, he went to Bible college and then seminary. He met the love of his life, Lola. They were married and started a family. It wasn't long until Fred was the pastor of a growing church.

After a few years, Fred and Lola were the parents of two beautiful daughters. However, he really wanted a son. So, he prayed, "Lord God, I have been a faithful servant to You. If it is Your will, let me have a son. And let him be a preacher of the gospel. And let him take the gospel around the world."

Fred prayed that prayer for several years. It began to look like he and Lola were not able to have any additional children, so they decided to adopt. They went through the process and were so blessed when they brought home a son. The family was sitting in the living room holding and admiring the baby when Lola spoke up. She said, "I've got more good news. I am going to have a baby."

Seven months later, she gave birth to another son. God gave Fred a double blessing. He now had two sons.

That was when Fred faced his crossroads. Back then, times were tough. It had been hard enough for Fred to make ends meet on his pastor's salary for a family of four. Now, with the two boys, they were a family of six. So, Fred decided to leave the ministry and go to work in the public school system. The pay and benefits were so much better. Fred knew at the time, God had called him to preach. He knew it was God's will for his life to serve in the church, but he decided to leave anyway. He quit his church and became a school administrator.

One day, Fred got a phone call at his office. Both baby boys were sick with a very high fever. Lola was taking them to the hospital.

When Fred arrived at the hospital, he was confronted with doctors who couldn't figure out what was wrong with his sons. Both boys were sedated. They had tubes running in and out of their little bodies. The situation did not look good.

Fred tried to comfort his wife. Then he walked down a hospital corridor to an empty chapel. Fred went down to the front of the chapel and knelt at the altar. Hot tears rolled

---

Did You Know?

Jonah spoke about there being mountains on the bottom of the sea (Jonah 2:6). That could not be proven in his day, but we know it is true today. We often think that Mount Everest (rising some 29,035 feet above sea level) is the tallest mountain on the planet. However, that honor belongs to Hawaii's Mauna Kea. Mauna Kea is only 13,796 feet above sea level, but it begins rising off the ocean floor nearly three and a half miles below the ocean's surface. Mauna Kea, when measured from the ocean floor, reaches a height of 31,796 feet. It is one of many mountains extending up from the ocean floor. We now know that there are mountains all over the ocean floor. Jonah declared long ago what modern science now understands to be true.

down his face as he talked to God. He said, "Lord, I am sorry that I have been out of your will. If you will just let my sons live, I will do whatever you want me to do. I will go wherever you want me to go."

Miraculously, the boys soon made a complete recovery. The doctors couldn't explain it. But both boys were released from the hospital after a couple of days.

Fred made good on his promise to God. He returned to serve as a pastor of a church. He served as a pastor for over sixty years. He served the Lord as a pastor right up until the day he died.

Neither of Fred's sons followed him in the ministry. But God answered his prayer for a son to be a preacher of the gospel in a different way. I was a young man when I walked into Dr. Fred Hambrick's church. I too had been running from God. But Fred recognized God's call in my life. He became my father in the ministry. He was my "Paul," and I was his "Timothy." He taught me. He poured his life into me. He became like another father to me. And God has used me to take the gospel of Jesus Christ around the world in fulfillment of Fred's prayer.

You are reading these words today because a fugitive who ran from God one day returned to God. Then that former fugitive found another fugitive and put him on the right path.

What path are you on?

Don't be a fugitive.

A Moment of Prophecy

According to Bible scholars, Jonah was a prophetic type of Israel, which, when called upon to preach the message of God's judgment and justice, refused to carry out the great commission. Because Israel refused to become a great witness to the world, God chose to punish them down through the centuries. God's punishment began some 3,000 years ago following the reign of King Solomon. Those three millennia seem to correspond to the three days Jonah spent in the belly of the fish. Many theologians believe that we are now at the closing days of those 3,000 years, and a time of the greatest judgment, the 7-year Tribulation is about to unfold on Israel.

CHAPTER 6

K.I.S.S.
Keep It Simple Saints

**He hath shewed thee, O man, what is good; and what
doth the LORD require of thee, but to do justly, and to love
mercy, and to walk humbly with thy God?**

—Micah 6:8

Several years ago, three brothers, Emmitt, Edgar, and Elmer,
went to a Christian men's retreat. While they were there,
they heard a sermon on wives submitting to their husbands.
They took that concept a little out of context. So, they went home and were
very assertive with their wives.

A few weeks later, the three brothers meet up for coffee on a Saturday
morning. As they talked, the conversation turned to how things were going
with their wives. The first brother, Emmitt, said, "I told my wife that I was
tired of helping her with housework. I told her that from now on she would
have to do all the cooking. The first day after I told her, I saw nothing. The
second day, I saw nothing. But on the third day when I came home from work,
the table was set, and she served a wonderful dinner—steak and potatoes. We
even had apple pie for dessert."

The second brother, Edgar, then spoke up. He said, "I sat my wife down and told her that from now on she would have to do her own shopping and do all of the cleaning. The first day, I saw nothing. The second day, I saw nothing. But on the third day when I came home, the whole house was spotless. Plus, the pantry shelves were filled with groceries."

Emmitt and Edgar looked over at their brother, Elmer. They asked him how things were going with his wife. Elmer sat up straight, pushed out his chest, and said, "I went home and gave my wife a stern look and told her that from now on she would have to do all of the cooking, all the shopping, and

> ## Micah
>
> **Contracted form of MICAIAH**
> וּהָיָכִימ **meaning "Who is like YAHWEH?" in Hebrew**

all the housecleaning. The first day, I saw nothing. The second day, I still saw nothing. But on the third day, the swelling went down, and I could see a little bit out of my left eye."

The point is, Elmer complicated the situation, and his wife had to un-complicate it. People tend to complicate things. Back in the 1960s, during the space race, the United States National Aeronautics and Space Administration (NASA) decided they needed a ballpoint pen to write in the zero-gravity when their space capsules were up in space. After much research and development, NASA developed the Astronaut Pen at a cost of approximately $1 million. The pen worked great. The Soviet Union was faced with the same problem. They just used a pencil. Sometimes we complicate things.

> ## Date
>
> **Micah prophesied in Judah through the reigns of Jotham (739–735 B.C.), Ahaz (735–715 B.C.), and Hezekiah (715–687 B.C.).**

One Sunday morning, a preacher was getting ready to deliver his message when he noticed on his sermon notes that his wife had written these letters: "K.I.S.S." He thought, "Oh, how sweet. She gave me a little kiss."

Right before he got up to preach, he said to his wife, "Thank you for the note. It was so sweet." She said, "It wasn't meant to be sweet. Those letters—K.I.S.S.—stand for 'Keep It Short, Stupid'!"

You have probably also heard K.I.S.S. stands for "Keep It Simple, Stupid." Since it is not nice to call people stupid, I decided to go a different route. Let's imagine that the letters, K.I.S.S. stand for "Keep It Simple, Saints."

The Bible calls Christians "saints." If you are a born-again, blood-bought child of God, then you are a saint. However, even saints complicate things. We especially complicate the Christian life. We have seminars, conferences, workbooks, videos, websites, books, and many, many resources that are designed to equip us to be strong believers.

If you go to any Christian bookstore, you will find titles such as *19 Principles for Christian Finances, 25 Tips to Have a Marvelous Christian Marriage, 150 Principles on How to Pray, 18 Godly Ways to Raise Your Kids,* and *17 Ways to Worship.* It seems as if we as modern Christians have moved away from the simplicity that was in the life of Jesus Christ.

Several years ago, I tried to learn to play golf. I spent a lot of money on a golf bag, golf clubs, golf balls, golf shoes, golf gloves, and golf shirts. I even bought a funny-looking, duck-billed golf hat. I had everything that I thought I needed to play golf except for the know-how. I had no idea how to play the game. However, I thought, "If I can overcome that obstacle, I will enjoy playing golf."

So, I asked a friend of mine to give me some tips. Bless his heart, he tried to teach me. In my mind, I thought golf was a simple game. I watched Tiger Woods on TV. Tiger just simply hit the ball with a club, and it flew through the air and landed near the hole. Then he walked up and tapped the ball in the hole. Simple, right?

One Saturday, my friend and I went out to the golf course for my lesson. He said to stand a certain way. He said to hold the club a certain way. He said to keep one arm straight. He said to slightly bend the other arm. He said to not grip the club too tight. He said to turn my neck a certain way. He said to tilt my head a little to the left. He said to bend my knees slightly. He said to rotate at the hips. He said to quit frowning. He said don't get frustrated …

All of that was just too much for me to remember. By the time we finished eighteen holes, I had a headache from the stress. Consequently, I decided that I didn't need to play golf anymore. It was way too complicated.

In the same way, we often complicate Christianity. I mean you must pray a certain way. You must say a certain thing. You must memorize a certain thing. You must worship a certain way. You can't even tell people about Jesus without memorizing a nineteen-point outline.

When the Lord Jesus Christ came to this Earth, His first followers were common, ordinary fishermen. Jesus said to those common, ordinary people, "Follow me and I'll make you fishers of men." Those common, ordinary people followed Jesus and they turned the world upside-down. I believe we need to get back to the simplicity of the early Christian church. We should keep it simple.

> ### *Did You Know?*
>
> **Micah was a contemporary of Isaiah, and their prophecies mirrored each other in several ways: both warned of a future exile in Babylon, both promised deliverance from Assyria, both prophesied that the Lord would raise up a son from the line of David to rule His people, both anticipated the exiles would return from Assyria and Babylon, and both spoke of Zion as the highest mountain on the Earth in the coming messianic Kingdom.**

A Working God

In the book of Micah, we find three reminders to help us keep it simple. First, we see a working God. God is working. Now that seems so simple, doesn't it? However, if we don't *see* God working, we don't *think* He's working.

Have you ever been in a church service where several people responded to the invitation? After that service, you might have said, "Wow! God was working in the church today!" However, what if nobody came forward publicly? Does that mean God was not working?

What about the husband and wife who were getting ready to divorce? As a last resort, they went to church, and the Lord gave them a word. Then they took each other by the hand and said, "We are not going to split up. We are going to work things out." Is that not God working?

What about the man who was thinking about giving up on life? Before he pulled the trigger, he went to church, and he got a word from God. Then he said, "I'm not going to kill myself. I'm going to get some help. I'm going to live for Jesus." Is that not God working?

What about new Christians who went to church to grow in their faith? Each week, God gave them a little nugget. Each week, they grew a little more in their faith. Is that not God working?

God is working even when we don't see Him working, but here in the book of Micah, the children of Israel forgot that God was working for them. So, God gave them a message.

Hear ye now what the LORD saith; Arise, contend thou before the mountains, and let the hills hear thy voice.

—Micah 6:1

Micah ministered to the Southern Kingdom of Judah during and after the fall of the Northern Kingdom to Assyria. Chapter six opens with a courtroom scene—the prophet pictures a court of law, with Judah "on trial" before the Lord. In the presence of unshakable witnesses (such as "the mountains" and "the hills" and the "strong foundations of the earth"), the court came to order. God said to His people, "Arise, plead your case"—and God brought His case, His complaint, against His people.

Micah 6 is like a scene from "Perry Mason," "Matlock," or "Law & Order." It is like a scene from a courtroom drama. The people are on trial, and the mountains are witnesses. The mountains have stood for many years in silence. In all those centuries, the mountains were witnesses to God working for His people. Micah said, "These mountains have watched God work. They stand as a silent faithful witness. If you don't think that God has been working on your behalf, tell these mountains where He failed you."

Hear ye, O mountains, the LORD's controversy, and ye strong foundations of the earth: for the LORD hath a controversy with his people, and he will plead with Israel.

—Micah 6:2

Micah made God's case against His people. At this time, the people had turned away from the Lord. They acted like there was no God. They forgot all about Him.

Have you forgotten about God? Have you forgotten all the times in your life that God has come through for you? If you are in a situation today, and you can't see God working, don't doubt God; don't question God; and don't complicate it by coming up with your own plans and schemes. Just simply remember all the times that God has come through for you.

Back during the closing days of World War II, one of America's mighty bombers took off from the island of Guam headed for Kokura, Japan. The plane was loaded with bombs to be dropped on that Japanese city. As the bomber got closer, the captain noticed the entire city covered in a cloud. He thought it unusual because the forecast called for clear skies.

Because clouds covered the target area, the sleek B-29 circled for nearly an hour until its fuel supply reached the danger point. The captain and his crew were frustrated because they were right over the primary target, but because of the clouds, they could not complete their mission. With their fuel running out, they finally decided to go for the secondary target. When they changed course, they found clear skies. The captain commanded, "Bombs away!" They destroyed their target, and the B-29 headed for home.

When they returned from their mission, the captain and his crew were greeted by a military intelligence officer who had just received some startling information. Just one week before the bombing mission, the Japanese transferred most of their captured Americans to the city of Kokura. Now, none of them knew this, but many of the Americans in the camp in Kokura were Christians. The believers in the camp organized a prayer vigil for God to work in their situation. If the clouds had not come up and protected the city, Kokura would have been destroyed and thousands of American men would have died.

God's ways are behind the scenes, but He moves all the scenes which He is behind. God is working, even when we can't see it.

A Weary Group

O my people, what have I done unto thee? and wherein have I wearied thee? testify against me.

—Micah 6:3

Even though God was working, His people were weary. Micah 6:3 is one of the saddest verses in the Bible. God asked His own people what He had done to make them weary.

Today, you are reading this, and you are weary. You are weary of God, weary of church, weary of reading the Bible, weary of being around other Christians. How can that be possible? You become weary when you forget to remember how God has worked in your life.

Did You Know?

The prophet Micah's name means, "Who is like the Lord," and the book ends with that exact same question, "Who is a God like you?" (Micah 7:18).

Again, the scene was like a courtroom drama. The people of God were on trial. The mountains were witnesses. God, acting as the prosecuting attorney, said, "Where is your evidence that I have failed you? Why have I made you tired?"

For I brought thee up out of the land of Egypt, and redeemed thee out of the house of servants; and I sent before thee Moses, Aaron, and Miriam.

—Micah 6:3

God's people were slaves in Egypt. Even though Pharaoh said, "I will never let you go," God delivered His people. God had worked in their lives, but they were weary waiting on God.

Aren't we the same today? We hate to wait for anything. I get frustrated waiting thirty seconds for a burrito to cook in a microwave. I stand in front of the microwave and yell, "Man, I wish that thing would hurry up!"

A Waiting Group

O my people, remember now what Balak king of Moab consulted, and what Balaam the son of Beor answered him from Shittim unto Gilgal; that ye may know the righteousness of the LORD.

—Micah 6:5

Do you remember the TV show "Mr. Ed"? Even if you don't remember the show, you probably remember the theme song:

A horse is a horse of course of course
And no one can talk to a horse of course.
That is of course unless the horse
Is the famous Mister Ed!

The TV show, "Mr. Ed," was about a talking horse. A talking horse makes for good television, but it is fiction. There is no such thing as a talking horse. However, there once was a talking donkey.

In the book of Numbers, Balak, the king of Moab, heard the armies of Israel had defeated all the armies that stood in their way. The Israelites had the Ark of the Covenant and the blessing of God. Balak realized he could not defeat the Israelites because God was on their side. So, he hired a prophet named Balaam to curse the army of Israel.

So, Balaam took his money, and he left on his faithful donkey. He was on his way to curse the people of God when an angel appeared. The angel stood in front of the donkey with a sword drawn. However, Balaam could not see the angel. Only the donkey saw the angel and he stopped. Balaam whipped the donkey, and he ran from side to side, but the donkey refused to move forward.

Finally, the donkey sat down. That was when Balaam started beating the tar out of the donkey. Then, the Bible says God gave the animal the ability to speak. The donkey turned around and said to Balaam, "Why are you beating me? Haven't I been a good donkey? Have I ever acted this way before?" Now here is the strange part: Balaam talked to the animal like it was a normal thing. He said, "You're right. You've never acted this way before." Suddenly, God opened the eyes of Balaam and he saw the angel with the sword standing there. God was working; Balaam just didn't see it. He wasn't watching.

You know, we don't know how many demon armies God has kept from us. We don't know how many times the devil was going to attack us and God stopped him. We just need to keep it simple and remember God is working, and then watch to see what he does.

By the way, the other day, we were coming home from church and I looked over at my wife and said, "Can you believe the way God is using me in the ministry?" She looked back at me and said, "I sure can. After all, if God can use a talking donkey, He can use you too!"

Anyway, we should watch and wait, but we have a hard time waiting on

God. We get frustrated and tired of waiting on God. Still, the Bible tells us over and over to wait on God. So, instead of spending your time waiting, try spending your time remembering.

Remember the day you got down on your knees and headed toward an old, rugged cross. Remember how you were headed to a burning Hell, but Jesus Christ saved you. Remember how you lost your job, but God provided you with another one. Remember how He saved your kid. Remember when you were so sick you didn't think that you were going to make it, but God pulled you through.

When you are waiting on God, don't just sit there being depressed. Remember how God has been good all these years and realize He will be again. Just keep it simple.

A Walk with God

If I could just sum up the Christian life in one sentence, it would be Micah 6:8: "He hath shewed thee, O man, what is good; and what doth the LORD require of thee, but to do justly, and to love mercy, and to walk humbly with thy God?"

Do justly. What does that mean? It means to treat people fairly. Do justly to people at work, at school, at church, at home. Treat others like you would like to be treated.

Did You Know?

Micah prophesied nearly seven hundred years before its fulfillment that the Messiah would be born in the town of Bethlehem in the region of Ephratah (Micah 5:2).

Love mercy. That means treating others with compassion. Be kind to people. Be nice. When that little girl knocks on my door to try and sell me some Girl Scout cookies right in the middle of my favorite TV Show, I'm going to treat her with loving-kindness. When the waitress messes up my order for the third time, I'm going to treat her with loving-kindness. When the kid at

Walmart can't seem to get the cash register to work and I must stand in line for twenty minutes, I'm going to treat him with loving-kindness.

Walk humbly. If you walk with God, that means you have fellowship with God. Surrender to God. Spend time with Him. Have friendship with Him. Walk humbly with God. Are you walking with God?

Back in the mid-1700s, there lived an old saintly woman who everyone called "Momma." Momma characterized Micah 6:8. She was just, loved mercy, and she walked humbly with God.

Momma was the lady that all the children in the neighborhood wanted as their mother. She had hair like a halo of silver, hands worn with calluses, and cheeks that were stained by tears. She cried tears for her son, Johnny. Every day and every night, you would find Momma crying and praying over her washtub in a room of poverty for her son Johnny.

Johnny left home as a rebellious teenager to become a sailor. In the years since, Johnny grew into an ungodly, wicked man who was disowned by his father and everyone who knew him. Still, day and night, Momma prayed that God would save, and use her wayward son.

One day, God answered the prayer of Momma by sending a storm. Johnny's ship was hit by a terrible and violent storm. Men washed overboard, and the ship was torn apart. During the storm, Johnny fell face down on the deck. He remembered many of the Bible verses that Momma taught him when he was a little boy. One of those passages said that whoever calls on the name of the Lord shall be saved. So, Johnny screamed. "Lord Jesus, save me." Miraculously, the storm stopped.

God answered Momma's prayer. The storm changed the direction of Johnny's life. He got saved, and Johnny, the drunken sailor, became John Newton the preacher, who wrote these words:

Amazing grace
How sweet the sound

That saved a wretch like me

I once was lost,

but now I am found,

Was blind, but now I see

John Newton's song, "Amazing Grace," has become one of the most influential and popular songs of all time. Some have called it the "Christian National Anthem."

Sadly, Momma Newton didn't live to see her son saved. However, because of her influence, the world has "Amazing Grace." We can sing "Amazing Grace" because of a believing, godly old mother, and her washtub prayers.

When you get up in the morning, why don't you ask God to walk close to you? Make it a daily habit to pray for the Lord to help you do justly; to help you love mercy; and to help you walk humbly in His presence. If you can do that, you will touch every life you meet.

Just keep it simple.

Keep It Simple, Saints.

A Moment of Prophecy

Micah speaks of the last days when the temple will be established on the "top of the mountains ... above the hills" (Micah 4:1–8). The mountain of the temple is Mount Zion. The Dome of the Rock, a Muslim shrine, is sitting upon the temple site today. The Romans used to dump their garbage on the temple site as an insult to the Jews. When the Muslims conquered Jerusalem, they discovered the Rock of Abraham under the huge pile of garbage and dung. They cleaned it off and built a shrine. The Rock of Abraham is sacred to Muslims because they believe Abraham offered up Ishmael there (not Isaac as our Bible states). They also believe Muhammad ascended into Heaven from the site. Despite the Dome of the Rock being on the site, the Bible says there will be two future temples: the Tribulation Temple that will be desecrated by the Antichrist, and the Millennial Temple where the Lord Jesus Christ will rule and reign over the planet.

CHAPTER 7

Prophets and Losses

The Lord is slow to anger, and great in power, and will not at all acquit the wicked: the Lord hath his way in the whirlwind and in the storm, and the clouds are the dust of his feet.

—Nahum 1:3

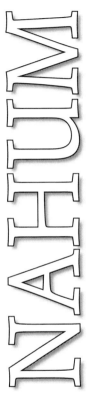

On January 14, 1919, a group of workers at the Purity Distilling Company in Boston, Massachusetts, complained to their manager, Arthur Jell. The workers were concerned about the safety of a molasses tank. They warned Jell they didn't believe the tank was structurally sound.

Molasses was very profitable in 1919. In addition to alcohol, fermented molasses was used to make dry powder, TNT, and other munitions for World War I. The immense size of the tank reflected the demand. It measured more than fifty feet high and ninety feet in diameter, and it Held two and a half million gallons of molasses. The tank, which had been built quickly, was leaking and making loud rumbling noises. However, Arthur Jell was

---

Nahum

Means "comforter" in Hebrew, from the root נחם **(nacham).**

more concerned about profits than safety. So, he ignored the warnings.

The next day, on January 15, 1919, at 12:40 in the afternoon, the huge tank ruptured. Like a tsunami, thirteen thousand tons of molasses flooded through the north end of Boston. Molasses is something like honey. It is a sugary-sweet product made from sugar cane. Molasses is ten thousand times denser than water. It is impossible to swim in sorghum molasses. Although rescuers were quick to arrive on the scene, vehicles and rescue workers on foot could barely get through the sticky goo that filled the streets.

Date

Nineveh fell before a combined assault of the Babylonians, Medes, and Scythians in 612 B.C. Nahum was written shortly before the destruction of Nineveh.

The great brown wave caught and killed most of the nearby employees of the Purity Distilling Company. Buildings were splintered. The local fire station was knocked off its foundation. A large truck was blasted through a large wooden fence. Homes, horses, and people were destroyed. A wagon driver was later found dead and frozen like a figure from the ashes of Pompeii.

How fast is molasses in January? The fifteen-foot-high wave moved at an estimated thirty-five miles per hour. The death toll began to rise and kept rising, day after day. Two bodies were found four days after the tank burst. They were so battered and glazed over by the molasses that identification was difficult. The final count was twenty-one dead, one hundred and fifty injured, and hundreds of horses killed. The molasses wave, after spreading out, covered several blocks of downtown Boston to a depth of two or three feet. Even today, over a hundred years later, the residents of north Boston insist that on warm summer days, the air is still tinged with the sweet smell of molasses.

Seven days before the flood, on a day when the temperature was two degrees Fahrenheit, a new shipment of half a million gallons of molasses was dumped into the poorly built tank. As the warm molasses mixed with the cold molasses in the tank, it triggered a fermentation process that produced gas. The twenty-six million pounds of molasses and the gas inside the tank put extra pressure on the steel walls which caused the rupture.

Sadly, the "Great Molasses Flood of 1919" could have been avoided. The Purity Distilling Company was warned. However, because of the motivation of profit, the warnings of a pending flood were unheeded.

Twenty-six hundred years ago, Nahum the prophet delivered a warning of a pending flood that also went unheeded. To understand Nahum's warning, we first need to go back to the book of Jonah. Nahum is a companion book to the book of Jonah because both prophets preached to the same city—Nineveh.

God sent Jonah to the city of Nineveh, the capital of the Assyrian Empire. Assyria was an enemy of Israel and would eventually overrun them, taking the nation into captivity. Nineveh was a place that was famous for being brutal, immoral, and idolatrous. Still, God sent Jonah with a warning. Then an amazing thing happened. All the city, from the king down to the poorest commoner—every person in the city of Nineveh—repented. They heeded God's warning from Jonah. Jesus Himself affirmed the validity of the repentance offered by this first generation of Ninevites (Matthew 12:41).

At the time of Nahum, a hundred years had passed since Jonah preached his message to Nineveh. After a hundred years, the people in Nineveh had forgotten God. The generation that repented died. The new generation of Ninevites returned to their old bloodthirsty ways of murder, adultery, fornication, and idolatry. They completely ignored the one true God. So, God sent Nahum to Nineveh to preach a message of certain judgment.

God's grace has limits. Jonah went to Nineveh and the city repented. However, the descendants of this generation proved to be unfaithful to God. Instead of continuing to honor the God of Israel, they chose rather to invade and conquer Israel in the latter part of that very same century. By the time Nahum came on the scene, Nineveh's wickedness had grown so great that Nahum described the city in the following manner: "Woe to the bloody city! it is all full of lies and robbery; the prey departeth not" (Nahum 3:1). Given these facts, it is perhaps best to understand Nahum's prophecy as a sequel to Jonah's prophecy. Jonah told of God's grace, but God's grace has limits and Nahum explains what happens when God's grace reaches those limits.

Did You Know?

In John 7:52, the Pharisees said, "... Search, and look: for out of Galilee ariseth no prophet." This was a lie. Jonah was from Galilee (2 Kings 14:25) and so was Nahum.

The people of Nineveh could not believe their city would ever be destroyed. When Nahum said, "I'm telling you that Nineveh is going to fall," the Ninevites never would have believed it. Nahum preached his message during the height of the Assyrian Empire when the fall of this powerful nation would have been inconceivable. As the Lord said through Nahum, "Thus saith the Lord; Though they be quiet, and likewise many, yet thus shall they be cut down, when he shall pass through. Though I have afflicted thee, I will afflict thee no more" (Nahum 1:12). God sent Nahum with a message for the Ninevites: Even though they were at full strength and many, they will be cut down.

Nineveh was a massive place—about seven miles in circumference. The city had two stone walls, an outer wall, and an inner wall. The inner wall was dotted with twelve hundred towers which were over two hundred feet high. The inner wall was fifty feet thick—wide enough for six chariots to race side by side. Nineveh was the most fortified city on Earth. So, when Nahum showed up and said, "God sent me to tell you that the end is near," it must have seemed laughable to the Ninevites.

However, the people of Nineveh did not know anything about the characteristics of God. So, Nahum told them about God. Today, people still don't know anything about the characteristics of God. So, I think it's important to understand some things we find in Nahum's prophecy about Almighty God.

God's Possessiveness Is Certain

First, Nahum tells us that God is possessive. Nahum says, *"God is jealous"* (Nahum 1:2). When he used the word "jeal-ous," he is not using it the way we use the word to describe the sin of jealousy. Sinful jealousy is mixed with envy. Somebody is jealous of what somebody else has and they will try to get it. It is an envious sinful atti-tude. However, that is not the jealousy of God. The word "jealous" here could be trans-

> ### Did You Know?
>
> **Nahum's book is only for-ty-seven verses long, and just like Obadiah's short prophecy, it is addressed to a foreign city.**

lated as "zealous" or "possessive." God is possessive over His people. God wants you.

As a husband, I am possessive for the love of my wife. I want to cherish that love. I want to protect her. I don't want anyone or anything to ever hurt her or take her from me. I have a zeal for my wife. Amanda and I started dating when she was a teenager. We have been together for decades, and I am still possessive for her after all these years.

Likewise, God is possessive for His people, He doesn't want any rivals as far as our relationship with Him is concerned. He doesn't want to share us with anybody, any idol, or any false god. He will never be satisfied for us to ignore Him or put Him on the back burner. God doesn't want third place. He's not even interested in second place. God wants first place in your life, and He doesn't want to share first place with anyone. God is possessive.

God's Punishment Is Certain

God is jealous, and the LORD revengeth; the LORD revengeth, and is furi-ous; the LORD will take vengeance on his adversaries, and he reserveth wrath for his enemies.

—Nahum 1:2

105

Not only is God's possessiveness certain, but His punishment is also certain. That is also found in Nahum 1:2 which tells us that God has wrath for His enemies. The Hebrew word for wrath describes hot, fiery anger.

Today, the wrath of God is seen as out of date. People don't want to hear about the wrath of God. So, today, most preachers never speak about the wrath of God. Today, most preachers preach only about the love of God. Now, it is true that God is a God of love, but He has wrath against sin. Most people believe the wrath of God is old-fashioned, but everything old-fashioned is not necessarily wrong or bad. Water is old-fashioned. It's been around since creation, but people still drink it. The Bible is old-fashioned, and it tells me that God is a God of wrath. He is a holy God who hates sin. Maybe I'm old-fashioned, but I believe if there was more Hell preached from the pulpit, there would be less Hell lived in the pews.

I think some of the problems people have with the idea of the wrath of God come from a wrong understanding of Jesus. Today, people have this idea that Jesus was a soft-spoken weakling. People say, "I just love the meek and lowly Jesus." They obviously don't understand that the meek and lowly Jesus had carpenter's hands. He was a man's man, who never cried out for mercy when he was beaten and crucified. The meek and lowly Jesus preached more about the fires of Hell than He did about Heaven.

The Bible says a day is coming when the meek and lowly Jesus will mount up on a horse. He will ride down here from Heaven. With a sword in His hands, and fire flashing from His eyes, He will stomp under His feet all the armies of this world. Then, the meek and lowly Jesus will cast the body and soul of every person who rejects Him as their only Savior into Hell.

However, I want you to understand that when Nahum speaks about God taking vengeance, it does not mean God is trying to get even with you. It means He executes justice. God gives people what they deserve. When a sinful person—and we are all sinners—refuses to repent and turn to the only Savior, Jesus Christ, then that sinner is under the wrath of God. They deserve punishment.

Unless that person turns to Christ, they will spend eternity in Hell.

God will punish His enemies. Nahum further described God's punishment When he wrote, "Who can stand before his indignation? and who can abide in the fierceness of his anger? his fury is poured out like fire, and the rocks are thrown down by him" (Nahum 1:6). The words "indignation" and "anger" speak of active anger. It's one thing to get mad and it's another thing to do something about the anger you're experiencing. The Bible says God is not just standing by like an angry spectator. When He sees people rejecting Jesus, He is not just going to stand on the sidelines and get mad. He will execute His anger by causing judgment to fall on the person who has not trusted Christ.

By the way, the word "fierceness" in Nahum 1:6 is a Hebrew word that means "burning." The word "fury" in the same verse means "heat." Don't tell me there is no burning Hell. The wrath of God is red hot.

One day, when I was in the eighth grade, we had a test in Mr. Alford's science class over the periodic table. I struggled to learn the periodic table. Who came up with those abbreviations anyway? Some of them made sense, like hydrogen. The abbreviation for hydrogen is H. Oxygen also has an easy abbreviation—O. Those make sense. However, some were very confusing. Take, for example, potassium. The abbreviation for potassium is K. There isn't even a K in the word potassium. The abbreviation for sodium is NA. I thought that meant "not applicable." Silver is abbreviated with the letters AG. I thought that was the abbreviation for "agriculture."

The periodic table left me confused. I was as lost as a goose in a snowstorm, so I decided to cheat. I took a clear plastic Bic ink pen, copied out the entire periodic table on a very small piece of paper, rolled the paper, and put it inside the pen. I planned to look at my periodic pen for the answers while taking the test.

My plan would have worked if not for my cousin Bubba. Bubba's real name was Jimmy Joe Jeff Johnny Paul Ray Elmer Junior, but that was a mouthful, so we just called him Bubba. Bubba was in Mr. Alford's science class with me. He sat in the desk right behind me on the day of the test.

At first, things went great. I filled in all the blanks on the test with the help of my periodic pen. Suddenly, Bubba whispered, "What's the abbreviation for mercury?" Since I didn't want to get caught, I tried to ignore him. But he persisted, "What's the abbreviation for mercury?" I still didn't answer. Finally, Bubba raised his hand and said, "Mr. Alford, my pen quit writing. Can I borrow James' pen?" That resulted in Mr. Alford taking the pen from me and escorting me out of the class to his office. It was a bad day after that.

I cheated, so there was a consequence. I was punished. There are consequences when you try to cheat your way through life without God. God is just, and because He is just, He must punish sin. His punishment is certain.

God's Power Is Certain

The Lord is slow to anger, and great in power, and will not at all acquit the wicked: the Lord hath his way in the whirlwind and in the storm, and the clouds are the dust of his feet.

—Nahum 1:3

Not only is God's possessiveness and punishment certain, but also His power is certain. In Nahum 1:3, he says God has His way in a whirlwind. In Oklahoma, where I come from, we would say, "The wrath of God is like a tornado."

Tornadoes are sudden, destructive, and very powerful. Even with all our modern technology and ways to predict the weather, tornadoes still slip by and kill hundreds of people each year. In 1999, from May 2 through May 8, Oklahoma had one hundred and fifty-two tornadoes that touched down. One hit on May 3, 1999, and it was the most powerful tornado ever recorded. The May 3 tornado caused over one billion dollars in damage.

Before the May 3 tornado hit, a man and his wife were sitting watching TV in their house in Moore, Oklahoma. The television said that there was a tornado on the way. So, the man and his wife ran to a nearby closet. As they were running, the house began to fly apart. They said it sounded like a freight train.

When the tornado hit their house, the house was destroyed. The only piece left standing was the area above the closet where the man and his wife were hiding and praying.

The Bible describes the wrath of God as being powerful. His wrath will be released suddenly and fiercely. God's judgment is coming like a deadly tornado.

Think about all the people who have never accepted Christ, and who live like there is no God. The Bible says that God's judgment is coming on those people like a tornado. Powerfully, swiftly, and suddenly judgment will fall on nonbelievers.

I remember reading about the famous French philosopher, Voltaire. Voltaire was a committed atheist, and he hated the Bible. In 1776, he predicted, "One hundred years from my day, there will not be a Bible on Earth except one that is looked upon by an

> ### Did You Know?
>
> **The book of Nahum contains some of the most eloquent, beautiful, and sophisticated poetry of the Old Testament.**

antiquarian curiosity-seeker." Well, the Bible is still here, but Voltaire is not. To those who have Voltaire's attitude, Jesus declared, "Heaven and earth shall pass away, but my words shall not pass away" (Matthew 24:35).

Anyway, Voltaire used to hold lectures against the Christian faith, calling it the "infamous superstition." He would often rip the pages out of the Bible, and he would throw the pages and the torn-up Bible at the audience. He said, "The Bible is not worth more than a twenty-five–cent novel." Then he yelled,

"Kill me, God. If there is a God, and He is a God of judgment, then judge me. Kill me."

In 1778, Voltaire became very ill. He said to his physician, "I will give you half of what I am worth if you will give me six months of life." When he was told this was not possible, he said "Then I shall die and go to Hell!"

When Voltaire died, it took seven nurses and three doctors to hold him down on the bed. He ripped his hair out, and cried, "Somebody pray for me. I don't want to go to Hell." Those were Voltaire's last words. After he died, his nurse said, "For all the money in Europe, I wouldn't want to see another unbeliever die! All night long he cried for forgiveness."

Judgment came for Voltaire. The Bible is clear if you die without Christ, then judgment is coming. You can't escape it. It is certain.

God's Patience Is Certain

Despite the certainty of God's judgment, He is patient. Nahum said, "The LORD is slow to anger" (Nahum 1:3). God is patient. He gives opportunities to repent. For the people of Nineveh, it had been a hundred years since Jonah preached, but God still sent them this preacher Nahum.

Maybe that is why God allowed you to pick up this book. God is slow to anger. We have all sinned and fallen short of the glory of God. We deserve Hell, but Christ on the cross took the fury and the wrath we should receive. Because Jesus took your Hell and your judgment, you can have life.

Just like the hand of God came down and protected the man and his wife who survived the May 3 tornado, God will protect you too if you come to Jesus. God's wrath will not fall on the Christian. Believers are washed and protected top to bottom by the precious blood of Jesus Christ.

Nahum continued that thought when he wrote, "The LORD is good, a stronghold in the day of trouble; and he knoweth them that trust in him" (Nahum 1:7). God is patient. He wants you to be saved. He doesn't want you to go to Hell. In fact, God won't send you to Hell. You'll send yourself there. God loves you so much that He has given you chance after chance to accept Christ. Yes, God is indeed patient, but His patience may be running out.

God promised He would destroy Nineveh and liberate Judah. God kept his promise, and the prophecy of Nahum was fulfilled in 612 B.C. when God sent the Babylonians to besiege Nineveh. The Babylonians surrounded the city of Nineveh for over two months. They eventually breached the walls and destroyed the city. Nineveh was brought to an abrupt end. Given its emphasis on the destruction of Nineveh, one of the questions raised by the prophecy of Nahum is, "What are we to make of it today?" Many view Nahum as a book that has no relevance for New Testament believers.

Well, we read in the New Testament that the Day of Judgment is fixed (Matthew 12:36; Acts 17:31; Romans 2:16; 2 Corinthians 5:10; Revelation 20:12). The clock is ticking. There are limits to God's grace. Jesus will by no means leave the guilty unpunished. He is the man appointed as the Judge of the world and He is coming to judge. Nahum's message is relevant for us today because Jesus is coming to judge and the time for repentance is growing short.

The message of Nahum is just as relevant today as it was in the seventh century B.C., because it reminds us that the time of God's grace is finite. It reminds us that the time to repent is now. It reminds us that the time to embrace Jesus is now. Just think about it for a moment. If invading the Northern Kingdom of Israel and deporting the people of God is an injustice which God meets with the swift and powerful judgment described in Nahum, what do you think he has in store for those who reject his only begotten Son?

You are living in the time of Jonah, but the time of Nahum is coming.

God's patience eventually ran out with Nineveh. We read in Nahum 1:8, "But with an overrunning flood he will make an utter end of the place thereof, and darkness shall pursue his enemies." About fifty years after Nahum spoke this prophecy against Nineveh, the city was destroyed. The Greek historian Ctesias in the fifth century B.C. records that while a drunken feast was going on, the gates of the city were swept away by a sudden rise of the river, and the palace foundations were dissolved. Archaeological evidence confirms a great flood destroyed walls and most of the city. Later, the enemies of Nineveh overran the city and killed all the flood survivors. Nineveh was destroyed so completely that "an utter end of the place" was literally made. The people and place of Nineveh were lost to history until the 1840s when the site was finally discovered by archaeologists.

Fifty years before it happened, God said He would destroy Nineveh with a flood. It wasn't a coincidence; it wasn't chance; it was the wrath of God that destroyed Nineveh.

Many years ago, there was an orphaned boy who lived with his grandmother. Their house caught fire and the grandmother ran upstairs to try to save the boy, but the staircase collapsed, and she died in the flames. As the flames grew closer to him, all the boy could do was cry and scream for help.

The boy's cries for help were finally answered by a man. The man climbed up an iron drainpipe and reached in the boy's bedroom window. Blindly, the man reached in through the smoke, the heat, and the flames, and he grabbed the little boy. With the boy hanging tightly to his neck, the man climbed back down the iron drainpipe.

Several weeks later, a public hearing was held to determine who would receive custody of the boy. A farmer, a teacher, and the town's wealthiest citizen all wanted the boy. The farmer spoke first. He said, "I can give the boy a good home. He will be fed and taken care of. He will learn the value of hard work and discipline by working on the farm."

The teacher then spoke. He said, "I have taught children for many years, but I have no children of my own. I will make sure this boy has the best education."

The wealthy man spoke next. He said, "I have made a fortune, but I have no heir. I have nobody to leave my wealth. I will give this boy a home and everything he could ever want."

As the men were talking, the little boy never looked at them. During the hearing, his eyes remained focused on the floor. He never looked up.

Suddenly, a stranger walked to the front of the courtroom and slowly took his hand from his pockets. His hands were burned and scarred. The people in the courtroom gasped, and the little boy smiled as he recognized the hands. This was the man who had saved his life. His hands had been burned when he climbed up and down the hot iron drainpipe.

The boy threw his arms around the man's neck and held on for dear life. The farmer turned and walked away. The teacher turned and walked away. The wealthy man turned and walked away. All silently walked away, leaving the boy and his rescuer alone. Those scarred hands settled the issue.

Two thousand years ago on a hill called Calvary, Roman soldiers drove nails into the hands of Jesus. Those nailed-scarred hands settled the issue.

How do you escape God's wrath? The nail-scarred hands of Jesus settled the issue. The Bible says, "He that believeth on the Son hath everlasting life: and he that believeth not the Son shall not see life; but the wrath of God abideth on him" (John 3:36). The one who believes in the Son will not suffer God's wrath for his sin, because the Son took God's wrath upon Himself when He died in our place on the cross (Romans 5:6–11). Those who do not believe in the Son, who do not receive Him as Savior, will be judged on the day of wrath (Romans 2:5–6).

Don't let His wrath fall on you.

A Moment of Prophecy

While Nahum was predicting the destruction of Nineveh, he also predicted that Judah would be spared. Nahum 1:15 says, "Behold upon the mountains the feet of him that bringeth good tidings, that publisheth peace! O Judah, keep thy solemn feasts, perform thy vows: for the wicked shall no more pass through thee; he is utterly cut off." Judah was indeed spared for a time. However, after one hundred and thirty-seven years, Judah became so idolatrous that God used the wicked city of Babylon to judge them. So, this prophecy will find ultimate fulfillment during the Millennium. Then the "wicked" will be "cut off;" consequently they "shall no more pass through" Judah.

CHAPTER 8

Myths of Modern-Day Revival

O Lord, I have heard thy speech, and was afraid: O Lord, revive thy work in the midst of the years, in the midst of the years make known; in wrath remember mercy.

—Habakkuk 3:2

Several years ago, an elderly man and his wife were driving across the country to visit some relatives. The wife was driving when she was pulled over by the highway patrol. The officer walked up to the driver's side of the car and said, "Ma'am, did you know you were speeding?" The patrolman didn't know it, but the woman was a little hard of hearing. So, she turned to her husband and asked, "What did he say?" He yelled, "He says you were speeding!"

The patrolman said, "May I see your license?" She turned to her husband again and asked, "What did he say?" He yelled, "He wants to see your license!"

She gave the officer her license. The patrolman then said, "I see you are from Oklahoma. I spent some time there many years ago and went on a blind date with the meanest, ugliest woman I've ever seen." She turned to her husband and asked, "What did he say?" Her husband yelled, "He thinks he knows you!"

The point is this: The woman didn't understand what the policeman was saying. For that matter, neither did her husband. Sometimes we don't understand what is being said, but when it comes to revival, we should have a good understanding. We should understand the biblical meaning of revival, but it is amazing how we misunderstand it. Revival is a word often spoken in Christian circles, but you might be shocked to learn that the word "revival" is not found anywhere in your Bible. However, the word "revive" is found in the Bible. The word "revive" is found in seven verses in the Word of God:

> ### Habakkuk
>
> From the Hebrew name חֲבַקּוּק (*Chavaqquq*), meaning "embrace" from the root חָבַק (*chavaq*)

1. "For thus saith the high and lofty One that inhabiteth eternity, whose name is Holy; I dwell in the high and holy place, with him also that is of a contrite and humble spirit, to *revive* the spirit of the humble, and to *revive* the heart of the contrite ones" (Isaiah 57:15).

2. "After two days will he *revive* us: in the third day he will raise us up, and we shall live in his sight" (Hosea 6:2).

3. "Though I walk in the midst of trouble, thou wilt *revive* me: thou shalt stretch forth thine hand against the wrath of mine enemies, and thy right hand shall save me" (Psalm 138:7).

4. "They that dwell under his shadow shall return; they shall *revive* as the corn, and grow as the vine: the scent thereof shall be as the wine of Lebanon" (Hosea 14:7).

5. "And he spake before his brethren and the army of Samaria, and said, What do these feeble Jews? will they fortify themselves? will they sacrifice? will they make an end in a day? will they *revive* the stones out of the heaps of

the rubbish which are burned?" (Nehemiah 4:2).

6. "Wilt thou not **revive** us again: that thy people may rejoice in thee?" (Psalm 85:6).

7. "O LORD, I have heard thy speech, and was afraid: O LORD, **revive** thy work in the midst of the years, in the midst of the years make known; in wrath remember mercy" (Habakkuk 3:2).

For several years, I misunderstood revival. I used to think revival was when lost people got saved, but that is evangelism, not revival. Revival is not when lost people get saved, but when saved people get right.

Evangelism is a work the church does for God, but revival is a work

Date
Habakkuk wrote his prophecy somewhere between 630 and 605 B.C.

God does for the church. Evangelism is an expression of the church; revival is an experience in the church.

The word "revive" means "to quicken," "to make alive." If you are a believer, God wants you to be alive. He wants you to be in a continuous state of revival. You might think revivals don't last. Well, the great preacher Billy Sunday once said, "They tell me a revival is only temporary; so is a bath, but it does you good." I agree. I think a revival would do us all some good, but we will not have revival until we get rid of the myths of modern-day revival.

The Contemporary Myth

The first myth that we need to get rid of is the contemporary myth. The contemporary myth says revivals are all old-fashioned. The contemporary myth is the belief that we can't have revival today.

Wilt thou not revive us again: that thy people may rejoice in thee?

—Psalm 85:6

The psalmist asked God, "Wilt thou not revive us again?" "Again" is a perpetual word. It applies right now. The word "again" means to restore or recover. Revival is not old-fashioned. God can send revival to us right here, right now.

Last year, my wife bought me a smartphone. The problem is the phone is smarter than me. It has every kind of app that you can imagine. My phone has a video player, recorder, camera, book reader, and a digital music player. There are apps on my phone that will let me play games, check my email, take my blood pressure, and pay my bills. It has a compass, clock, calculator, and calendar. It will even start my car. However, I can't work any of it.

All my contacts want to text me. Even that is beyond me. I don't Twitter and I don't text because my mouth works faster than my fingers do …

A while back, I was in Kansas on business for a week. While I was there, it snowed. My wife called, and I said the snow was beautiful. She asked me to send her a picture. By the time I figured out how to work the camera on my phone, the snow melted. I guess I'm just old-fashioned.

Still, just because something is old-fashioned, doesn't mean it's irrelevant for today. Food is old-fashioned. Since the Garden of Eden, people have needed food. Food is old-fashioned, but I still enjoy making my way to the kitchen two or ten times a day to get something to eat.

So, even if it is old-fashioned, revival is still relevant today. Our country needs an old-fashioned revival.

The Commitment Myth

Not only do we need to defeat the contemporary myth, but we also need to defeat the commitment myth. The commitment myth says, "I am far too busy to commit to attending church regularly." The commitment myth says, "I don't want to commit to a local church."

> **O LORD, I have heard thy speech, and was afraid: O LORD, revive thy work in the midst of the years, in the midst of the years make known; in wrath remember mercy.**
>
> —Habakkuk 3:2

Habakkuk was a Levite. Not much is known about him apart from the book that bears his name. However, we do know about the time in which he lived. The condition of Habakkuk's day was one of helplessness and hopelessness. The nation of Judah was going through a time of desolation and destruction. The only hope that the people had rested in revival.

In Habakkuk 3:2, the prophet asked God to "revive thy work in the midst of the years." The phrase, "in the midst of the years" means "God interrupt our day-to-day activities." In other words, Habakkuk asked God to send a revival and interrupt what they were doing. God's people were so busy with their everyday lives that they didn't have time to commit to God.

Several years ago, I was traveling to Fort Hood, Texas, and I had a layover in the Dallas airport. I made my way to the connecting gate and sat down. I looked up at a man walking toward me. He asked if anyone was sitting in the seat next to me. When I said no, he sat down. I noticed that before he sat down,

> ### *Did You Know?*
>
> **Habakkuk is an unusual prophetic book in that it does not directly address the nation of Israel. Instead, it is a dialogue between the prophet and the Lord followed by a lament and a psalm.**

he had a difficult time getting around. He walked with a cane in one hand and his oxygen tank on wheels in the other. He wore an oxygen mask and struggled to breathe.

I also noticed that the man was a fan of the Dallas Cowboys. He wore Dallas Cowboys clothes. He had on a Dallas Cowboys shirt, a Dallas Cowboys jacket, a Dallas Cowboys hat, and he even had Dallas Cowboys stars on his shoes. There was a Dallas Cowboys bumper sticker on his oxygen tank.

The man said that he was going home from a Dallas Cowboys pre-season team workout event of some kind. Before I could get a word in, he told me all about his love for and devotion to the Dallas Cowboys. He said, "I am a season ticket holder. I buy two season tickets—one for me and one for my canister." He smiled and pointed to his oxygen tank. He said, "I never miss a game. I fly down and spend two nights at the hotel. I come in a day early and I stay a day late. I am here in the rain. I am here in the sunshine. I am here when it is hot. I am here when it is cold. I never miss a game. I will do anything for my Dallas Cowboys."

As the man spoke, I couldn't help but think, "Wouldn't it be wonderful if we just had a small percentage of Christians that had that attitude about Jesus?" Wouldn't it be great if we had an attitude that said nothing is going to stop me from keeping my commitment to the Lord?

Do you know why churches in America struggle to have revival? It's because empty seats can't have revival. We must set aside some time for God. If we will set aside time each week for God and give God one hundred percent, there is no telling what will happen in this country.

I heard about a pastor who called people who visited his church. One day, he called a number and a young voice answered the phone with a whisper, "Hello."

The pastor said, "Who is this?"

The voice on the other end quietly replied, "This is Jimmy."

"How old are you, Jimmy?" the pastor asked.

"Four," Jimmy whispered.

"Jimmy, may I please speak to your mom?"

"She's busy."

"Can I speak to your dad?"

"He's busy too."

"Well, are there any other adults at your house?"

"The police."

"Well, let me speak to one of the police officers."

"They are busy."

"Who else is there?"

"The firemen."

"Put one of the firemen on the phone."

"They are busy."

The pastor was concerned and asked, "Jimmy, what are all those busy people doing?"

Jimmy giggled and in a hushed voice said, "They're looking for me."

Now that's a funny story, but the truth is we are busy people living in a busy world. We are so busy that we don't have time for God. A recent survey showed only eleven percent of Americans read the Bible daily. Less than half of all people in the United States pray one or more times a week. Another poll showed less than thirty-seven percent of Americans regularly attend church services. Americans are too busy to spend time with the Lord.

Habakkuk preached to busy people. His solution was to pray for God to interrupt their lives and send a revival. I wonder what would happen if just a few committed Christians prayed a prayer like that for America. Wouldn't it be wonderful if God were to "revive thy work in the midst of the years?"

The Complacent Myth

In addition to the contemporary myth and the commitment myth, we also need to defeat the complacent myth. The complacent myth says, "I'm a good person. I don't need revival."

Chapter 3 of Habakkuk is a prayer. Habakkuk tells us it is a prayer in the first verse which reads, "A prayer of Habakkuk the prophet upon Shigionoth." The Hebrew word translated "prayer" means "to beg and plead." It comes from a word that means "to sweat and perspire." The imagery is of a person who agonizes in the presence of God. The word *Shigionoth* means "with strong emotion." Thus, the prophet poured out his soul to God "upon [according to] Shigionoth," or according to the pain that he felt for his people. Habakkuk was begging, pleading, and agonizing with strong emotion for God to send revival.

Do you know why Habakkuk prayed that way? It was because his nation was in trouble. Habakkuk prayed and pleaded because God's judgment was about to fall on his nation. The nation of Judah had become complacent, but they were in desperate need of revival.

Have you ever been to a complacent church? Complacency has killed many American churches. I have been in some churches that were deader than a government job at four in the afternoon.

I preached in a church where the congregation looked like they had been drinking pickle juice. They showed up on Sunday morning, and they sat with their arms folded with a sour look on their face. It was like they were saying, "Bless me if you can, preacher. A lot better than you have tried and have never done it." It was a dead church. I am talking about a bona fide, take a pulse, on a respirator dead church.

The people at that dead church challenged me. I was a young and inexperienced preacher. I didn't know any better, and I believed people went to church to praise God, to hear the Word of God, and to love Jesus. I was just excited to preach. However, that church was deader than a hammer.

During the music, I was the only one who sang. Everybody else grunted and looked around. One lady sat there and read *People Magazine*.

I stepped up in the pulpit to preach, and I heard a noise. I looked up and saw a man fall out of the pew. He fell asleep and fell over. He just lay on the floor and snored.

Now you may not be part of a dead church, but couldn't everybody use a fresh touch from God? Have you grown complacent in your faith?

When was the last time you had a sweet hour of prayer? When was the last time you read the Bible, and it was like a fresh love letter—it was like God speaking to you? When was the last time you listened to a gospel hymn, and you just burst out in thanksgiving to God? When was the last time that you just walked and talked with God? Everybody needs a fresh touch from God. We all need revival.

Disobedient People Need Revival

The Bible tells us that disobedient people need revival. Habakkuk says, "… in the midst of the years make known; in wrath remember mercy" (Habakkuk 3:2). The prophet knew God's judgment was about to fall on Judah. Why? Because God's people were disobedient.

I am not a prophet, nor the son of a prophet. However, God's judgment is certain to fall on America. In fact, I believe His judgment is already falling on America. We are getting exactly what we deserve.

Think about where we are today. Society has kicked God out. Sinners have raced out of the closet while the church got quieter and hid in the closet. Men are allowed to marry men and women are allowed to marry women. We build more jails each year than we ever have while three thousand churches close their doors each year. Divorce has destroyed the family. We have murdered a whole generation and called it a choice. Transgendered perverts are permitted to share the same bathroom as my wife and daughter. Could it be the judgment of God is already on America?

Defiled People Need Revival

In addition to disobedient people, defiled people also need revival. In 2 Samuel 11, we read about how David committed adultery with Bathsheba. Then, to cover up his sin, he basically murdered Bathsheba's husband. Later, David repented, and wrote about his sin in Psalm 51:10 where he used a word that is very close to the word "revive." It is from the same Hebrew family. David cried and said, "Create in me a clean heart, O God; and renew a right spirit within me" (Psalm 51:10). The word "renew" is very close to the Hebrew word "revive." It comes from a word that means "to repair." David's life was broken from sin. So, David said, "God fix or repair me."

> **Did You Know?**
>
> Habakkuk's name means "to embrace" or "to cling." Through his prayerful interaction with God, Habakkuk learned to cling to God by faith.

> **Did You Know?**
>
> Many scholars believe that Habakkuk 3 was a prayerful song —a prayer set to music. The word "prayer," in Habakkuk 3:1 is the Hebrew word *palal*, which means "a hymn of intercession." This prayer of Habakkuk was a spiritual song, birthed by the Holy Spirit, as a cry that He would use to produce revival.

If there is one thing the modern church needs, it is a revival of holiness; a revival of purity; a revival that reminds us that we are not better than the world, but rather we are separated from the world and our standards are not the standards of the world.

Sadly, most people in the church today are like the little boy who knelt by his bed and prayed, "God, I want to be good. Now, not too good—just good enough to not get a spanking." That's how most of us live.

Most church people today would say that they are basically good. They believe themselves to be a good person. They would never steal. They would never be called a thief. But many of them don't tithe. They don't give to the work of the Lord. The Bible says that is stealing from God. It's sin.

Most church people today would never tell a big ole ugly lie. They would never tell a big ole black lie. However, they just tell those little bitty white lies. It's sin.

Most church people would never commit adultery. Yet they allow a lot of things on their computer screen and TV that are not Christ-like. It's sin.

Most church people would never murder. They would never hurt a soul. However, Jesus said if you hate someone, that is the same as murder. It's sin.

Discouraged People Need Revival

Not only do disobedient and defiled people need revival, but also discouraged people need revival. There is a familiar passage over in the Book of Isaiah 40:31 that speaks about this truth. The Bible says, "But they that wait upon the LORD shall renew their strength; they shall mount up with wings as eagles; they shall run, and not be weary; and they shall walk, and not faint." Did you notice the word "renew" again? Here "renew" means "to be rebuilt." It means to gain strength.

I am going to be honest. Sometimes, I get discouraged. My career in the U.S. Army has left my body in constant pain. My bones ache and there is a constant ringing in my ears. The ministry places more demands on me than I have time to complete. There are days when I get run down and it feels like I am running on fumes. Most mornings, I want to just call in sick and stay in bed.

Not too long ago, I was feeling discouraged. That day, I walked into a little church where a woman was playing the piano and a man was singing. They were just playing, singing, and praising the Lord. When I stepped into the back of that church, I knew I was standing on holy ground. I felt the glory of God in that place.

I just sat in the back and listened. Suddenly it hit me—it was like God spoke to me. It was like God said, "Some people in My church are already in revival. Why aren't you in revival?"

I am an evangelist. I am a preacher. I am supposed to be God's man, but I still needed revival. So, there in the back of that little church, I just started praying and praising God. Suddenly all my discouragement was gone. I got revived.

Do you know who may need revival today? It may be a good teacher. It may be a good worker. It may be a leader in the church. It may be someone who does all they can for God—but they need a fresh touch from God. However, God won't do it until you come to a place where you say, "God, I am complacent. Wake me up and revive me."

The Costly Myth

In addition to the contemporary myth, the commitment myth, and the complacent myth of modern-day revival, there is also the costly myth of modern-day revival. The costly myth says that revivals are over and you will never have another one.

Dr. John MacArthur recently said that we in America have had our last genuine move of God. He said we will have drops of mercy here and there, but we are in the last days. We are in the falling away age.

Francis Chan, the author of the best-selling Christian book *Crazy Love,* recently said, "God didn't say in the last days there would be revival. He said that in the last day's people will not put up with sound doctrine."

Respectfully, I disagree with John MacArthur and Francis Chan. While I do believe we are living in the last days, I still believe in revival.

Do you remember the 1960s? The 1960s was a time of upheaval and stress in America. We were in a war that we didn't want to be in. The economy was in despair. Murders were on the rise. Drug use was sweeping the nation. It sounds an awful lot like today, doesn't it?

Right at the end of the 1960s, there came a surprise. It was called the Jesus Movement. The Jesus Movement started in California when some Baptist missionaries shared the gospel with two hippies who got saved in the Haight Ashbury district of San Francisco. The two hippies opened a coffee shop, and they started preaching and sharing the gospel with their customers. From that little coffee shop, the Jesus Movement grew, and it swept the nation.

Time Magazine did a cover story and called the young people in the Jesus Movement "Jesus Freaks." Their symbol was a hand with one finger pointing up: One way to God, Jesus. Thousands were saved, and thousands were revived. Billy Graham called the Jesus Movement a genuine movement of the Holy Ghost.

Back when the Jesus Movement was going on, one Sunday night in 1970, a Baptist Church in Houston, Texas, held a routine service. It was the same time. It was the same place. It was the same format. It was the same preacher. It was the same people.

When the preacher gave the invitation that night, a young lady came forward. She walked down the aisle and she said, "Preacher, I want to get right with God. I want to confess my sins to the Lord. I want to repent right here in front of the church."

When the young lady stood up and repented, the Holy Spirit of God fell on the church in revival. People started to pour out of the pews. They began to seek God in repentance.

People left the church, went home, got friends and family, and brought them back. The church soon became packed with people who were seeking

God in prayer. The church was so full, that many stood in the door looking in because there was no room. Another invitation was given, and more people were saved and many more were revived.

After a few hours of prayer, the congregation sent some people to the education building next door to relieve the couple that had been over there taking care of the kids. The couple entered the sanctuary and said, "We have a grown son. He has left home, and he is far away from God. We don't even know where he is. Will you all please pray that God will get a hold of him?"

At that moment, their son was in Galveston at a party. When the people

in that church in Houston got on their knees and began to pray for their son, the Holy Spirit fell on him. God said to his heart, "Go home." So, he jumped in his car, and he drove back to Houston as fast as he could go. He first went to his parent's house, but to his surprise, they were gone. He decided to go get a hamburger. As he drove to the Dairy Queen, he passed the church. He noticed the lights were on, and the parking lot was packed with cars. Then he saw his parent's car, and all the people standing at the doors looking inside.

He parked, got out, and walked to the church entrance. He asked a man, "Where are my folks?" The man pointed down to the altar. The young man walked down the aisle and tapped his parents on the shoulder. They were amazed to see their son. He looked at them and said, "I felt God speaking to me. I'm coming back home, and I'm coming back to God."

Someone reading this may be thinking that was a long time ago. It was just in 1970. People still had to go to work and school the next day. Still, that church service didn't end until past ten that night. People kept getting saved and people kept getting revived. Nobody wanted to go home because those times are rare. Those times are precious.

I don't know about you, but I want my kids and grandkids to grow up with experiences like that. I want young people to leave church each week knowing they have been with God. I want all of us to know we have been in a place where only God can do what's going on. I want all of us to see the glory of God fall right here in America.

Some have said America can't have revival. Maybe not, but *you* can have revival. Draw a circle and get inside and ask God to do a fresh work in your life beginning right here and right now.

A Moment of Prophecy

Habakkuk prophesied of the Second Coming of Jesus Christ when he wrote, "God came from Teman, and the Holy One from mount Paran. Selah. His glory covered the heavens, and the earth was full of his praise. And his brightness was as the light; he had horns coming out of his hand: and there was the hiding of his power" (Habakkuk 3:3-4). This vision of the glorified Lord will have its literal fulfillment with the glorious appearing of Christ upon the Earth and the setting up of His kingdom (see Revelation 19:11-16; 21:23).

ZEPHANIAH

CHAPTER 9

Hide-and-Seek

Seek ye the LORD, all ye meek of the earth, which have wrought his judgment; seek righteousness, seek meekness: it may be ye shall be hid in the day of the LORD's anger.

—Zephaniah 2:3

David Cerqueira is a pediatrician in South Texas. A while back, Dr. Cerqueira shared Sarah's story with a group of Christian men. I heard the story and wanted to share it here with you. It all started several years ago when David's wife, Anna, who is a Sunday school teacher in their church, prepared a lesson on being useful. She taught the children that everyone could be useful—that usefulness was serving God and doing so was worthy of honor. The kids in her class sat and quietly soaked up her words. When the lesson ended, there was a short moment of silence. A little girl named Sarah spoke up. She said, "Teacher, what can I do? I don't know how to do any useful things."

Anna quickly looked around and spotted an empty flower vase on the windowsill. She said, "Sarah, you can bring a flower and put it in the vase. That would be a useful thing." Sarah frowned and said, "But that's not important." Anna said, "It is if you are helping someone."

The class ended, and the children left. The next Sunday, Anna was surprised when Sarah brought in a dandelion and placed it in the vase. This became Sarah's routine. She continued to bring a dandelion each week. Without reminders or help, Sarah made sure the vase was filled with a bright yellow flower, Sunday after Sunday.

So, what does Sarah's story have to do with the prophet Zephaniah? In the book that bears his name, Zephaniah warned the people of God how to prepare their lives before the wrath of God came. One of the ways the people were to prepare was to order their lives around humble service, and Sarah's story is an example of humble service.

Have you ever played the game hide-and-seek? When I was a kid, we used to play hide-and-seek all the time. In the game hide-and-seek, one kid would be "it." He would be the seeker. The rest of us would be the hiders. The kid who was "it," the seeker, would close his eyes and he would count to twenty. While he was counting, the rest of us would run and hide. Then the person who was "it," the seeker, would yell, "Ready or not, here I come." Then he would go out and try to find where everybody was hiding. Do you remember playing hide-and-seek?

Well, in some ways, the child's game hide-and-seek describes how we live our lives. We either seek after God or we hide from God.

> **Seek ye the LORD, all ye meek of the earth, which have wrought his judgment; seek righteousness, seek meekness: it may be ye shall be hid in the day of the LORD's anger.**
>
> —Zephaniah 2:3

Zephaniah said all those who seek the Lord will be hidden from the Lord's anger. He promised that those who humbly responded to God's offer of forgiveness would be spared the full brunt of His wrath. The expression, "ye shall be hid" is a wordplay on the prophet's name.

Zephaniah's name means, "the Lord hides or protects." When God hides His people, they are completely protected from harm.

Zephaniah was the great-great-grandson of King Hezekiah. He came from royalty. Zephaniah was God's prophet to the people during the reign of King Josiah. During that time, the people of God were going through a revival. They were turning back to God.

Zephaniah wrote his book in about 630 B.C. It is a short book—only three chapters. Chapter one is about the Day of the Lord. Chapter two is about God's judgment. Chapter three is about how God will be merciful to His people if they turn back to Him.

The book of Zephaniah follows the Four R's pattern often found in the teachings of the prophets of Israel. The Four R's pattern are Rebellion, Retribution, Repentance, Restoration. First, the people *rebel* against the teachings of the Lord. Second, the Lord exacts *retribution* or judgment against them. Third, the people see the error of their ways and *repent,* or "turn away" from evil. Fourth, when the people finally see the error of their ways and repent, then the Lord is able (and willing) to *restore* fully.

It seems to me God's people would be better off if they just obeyed God in the first place. Life would be much better if we followed a One R pattern: Resist—*resist* sin. However, if you read the Bible, you will find repeatedly that God said this is what you're supposed to do, and the people don't listen, and they don't obey. Over and over, we find in the Bible God saying, "Here is what I want you to do." However, the people ignored Him and did what they wanted to do.

Date

Zephaniah prophesied during the reign of Josiah in Judah (637-607 B.C.).

Why is it we have a hard time following directions? The directions seem so simple, so obvious, but we don't follow them. That is why we must put stupid warning labels on products to protect us from ourselves. The other day, I read a label on a bottle of milk that said, "Warning: After opening, keep upright ..."

Here are a few more warning labels. I found on a package of peanuts: *Warning: Contains Peanuts*. I read on a gas tank: *Warning: Never use a lit match or an open flame to check fuel level*. There is a label on our washing machine that says: *Warning: Do not put a person in this washer*. On a can of Scrubbing Bubbles toilet bowl cleaner there was this label: *Warning: Do not use for personal hygiene*.

> ### Did You Know?
>
> **Zephaniah's name means "the Lord shelters or protects" and it aptly summarizes a major theme of the book (Zephaniah 2:3; 3:12).**

Our kids like the Jell-O Pudding that comes in those little plastic cups. On one of those was a label that said: *Warning: Product will be hot after heating*. On an iron there was this label: *Warning: Do not iron clothes on body*. Still, my favorite was this one on my chainsaw: *Warning: Do not try to stop chain with hands*. Do we really want someone using a chainsaw that needs those kinds of instructions?

God's Word gives us warning labels that are simple and obvious, but what do we do? We don't follow the directions.

Seek the Heavenly Father

God gave Zephaniah a warning label with three simple and obvious directions. He tells us three things we should seek. First, we should seek the Heavenly Father. Zephaniah 2:3 begins with the words, "Seek ye the LORD." In other words, seek your Heavenly Father. That sounds obvious, but most of the time, our lives don't reflect that we are seeking the Lord. Instead, we hide from the Lord. Our goals, wants, and desires take over and that becomes what we seek instead of seeking the Lord.

Have you ever gone back and looked at your high school yearbook? I came across mine a while back. In my yearbook, they asked a question: What do I want to do in the next twenty years? They printed the answer in the yearbook next to your picture.

What did my class want to do in the next twenty years? One kid said he wanted to make a million dollars. Another said he wanted to achieve All-American Honors and play professional baseball. One girl said she was going to be a rock star. One guy said he was going to rob a bank and escape to Fiji. A girl said she would finish medical school and have a practice. Another said she would marry a rich movie star and live in Beverly Hills. Someone said they would travel around the world. One person said that he would live fast, die young, and leave a good-looking corpse.

The kids in my high school had all sorts of goals. Some were admirable; others were questionable. What are you trying to become in life? Whatever you seek in life can sometimes pull you away from seeking the Lord.

What does it mean to "seek the Lord?" The Bible says in Psalm 119:10, "With my whole heart have I sought thee: O let me not wander from thy commandments." The Bible also says, "But if from thence thou shalt seek the LORD thy God, thou shalt find him, if thou seek him with all thy heart and with all thy soul" (Deuteronomy 4:29).

To "seek the Lord" is to seek a relationship with the Heavenly Father. It's a path you choose to take you closer to God. It's about being obedient. It's about following God's commandments in the Bible.

Everybody reading this is seeking after something. Some seek fame. Some seek recognition. Some seek money. Some seek a career. Some seek a relationship with another person. But are you seeking after the Lord? Are you seeking after your Heavenly Father?

I read about this man who was a corporate headhunter. His job was to find executives for big companies. When a company lost an executive, that company hired this headhunter to search and find an executive to put in that vacancy.

The headhunter had an unusual way of screening executives. He sat down with the executive. He took off his jacket and tie. He worked to make the executive relax and feel comfortable. He talked about football and their families. When he believed they were calm and relaxed, the headhunter leaned in and asked, "What is your purpose in life?" Over the years, he was amazed at how many executives just fall apart at that question. They couldn't answer it. It left them speechless.

> ### Did You Know?
>
> **Zephaniah was the last of the twelve minor prophets to write before the captivity. He warned of the coming judgment—the coming time of wrath upon the disobedient Jewish people.**

However, there was one exception. Once, the headhunter took an executive to dinner. He talked about sports and his family. Then he leaned in and asked, "Bob, what is your purpose in life?" Bob said, "To go to Heaven and take as many people with me as I can." The headhunter said for the first time in his life, he was speechless.

If somebody asked you, What is your purpose in life? What would you say? What do you seek? Are you seeking after the Lord? Are you seeking after your Heavenly Father?

Seek Holiness

Not only must we seek after our Heavenly Father, but we must also seek holiness. Zephaniah 2:3 says, "Seek ye the LORD, all ye meek of the earth, which have wrought his judgment; seek righteousness." The word "righteousness" means "holiness." It means doing what is right.

God is the standard for holiness. If you ask someone if they are a good person, most people will say, "Yes." However, they are comparing themselves to a criminal. They think, "Well, I am not a murderer. I am not a rapist. I am not a thief. I am a good person." However, the Bible teaches that we should not compare our holiness to the holiness of other people, but to the holiness of God. God's holiness is the mark. Our goal is to be more like Jesus. It is an everyday journey of seeking holiness in our lives.

What does seeking holiness do for you? The Bible says in Matthew 5:6, "Blessed are they which do hunger and thirst after righteousness: for they shall be filled." As you seek after righteousness or holiness, you will be filled with satisfaction.

Where do you go to find God's standard for holiness? The Bible says in 2 Timothy 3:16, "All scripture is given by inspiration of God, and is profitable for doctrine, for reproof, for correction, for instruction in righteousness." God's Word, the Bible, is the tool for training ourselves in righteousness or holiness.

Chet Atkins was a legendary musician and producer who created the "Nashville Sound" in the 1950s and '60s. He was also one of the greatest guitar players that ever lived. He played guitar on just about every record that came out of Nashville in the 1960s. Over his lifetime, he won fourteen Grammys and sold millions of albums. His guitar playing earned him a spot in both the Country Music and Rock and Roll Halls of Fame. In fact, Chet Atkins' nickname was Mr. Guitar.

> ### Did You Know?
>
> **Zephaniah was a contemporary of the well-known prophet Jeremiah.**

Well, when Chet Atkins was seventy years old a reporter asked him a question. The reporter asked, "Mr. Atkins, you are seventy and the greatest guitar player that ever lived. Why do you still practice six hours a day?" Chet answered, "Because I think I'm making progress."

It is the same way in your Christian life. Your goal should be to make progress every day. You should be a better Christian today than you were yesterday.

It's like exercising your body. Exercise is supposed to be ongoing training. You can't wake up one day and say, "I have decided to get in shape, so I am going to exercise today," then expect to be done. The first day of a new exercise program just shows you how out of shape you really are. The same is true of holiness, but you must keep working to be more like Jesus every single day.

Seek Humility

In addition to seeking the Heavenly Father and holiness, we also must seek humility. Zephaniah said, "... seek meekness: it may be ye shall be hid in the day of the Lord's anger" (Zephaniah 2:3b). The word "meekness" means "humility."

I knew a guy who said, "I like to think of myself as a humble man." Once you got to know him, you would realize he just liked to think of himself. Humility is a rare trait in our world today.

Have you ever known anybody that thought more of others than they did of themselves? Have you ever known anybody that was always lifting other people up? Have you ever known anybody who selflessly served others?

The greatest example of humility was the Lord Jesus Christ. The Bible tells us that on the night before Jesus was crucified that He took a basin of water and a towel, and He washed and dried the feet of His disciples. The God of the universe washed the nasty, dirty, stinky feet of His disciples to teach them a lesson on how to serve one another. He washed their feet to teach them a lesson on how to be humble.

The humility of Christ was also shown on the cross. We read in Philippians 2:8, "And being found in fashion as a man, he humbled himself, and became obedient unto death, even the death of the cross." He served us by taking the sins of the world—your sins and my sins—to the cross.

Jesus died in agony and shame on an old, rugged cross as an act of humble service. That should motivate all believers to humbly serve Him. How can we do that? We can be a blessing to others.

I started this chapter by sharing a story told by Dr. David Cerqueira about a little girl named Sarah. Sarah blessed others by bringing a dandelion to her Sunday school class every week. David's wife, Anna, was Sarah's Sunday school teacher. Anna was so blessed, she told their pastor about Sarah's faithfulness.

The pastor then moved the vase from Anna's Sunday school classroom to the main sanctuary right next to the pulpit. The next Sunday morning, there was a dandelion in the vase. The pastor preached a sermon about the honor of serving others. He used Sarah's flower as an example.

> **Did You Know?**
>
> **The phrase "the day of the Lord" occurs seven times in Zephaniah and is alluded to nineteen other times.**

Many people in the church were touched by the message, and that week started on a good note.

However, that same week, Dr. Cerqueira got a call from Sarah's mother. She was worried that Sarah seemed to have less energy than usual, she didn't have an appetite, and she didn't want to play. Dr. Cerqueira made room in his schedule to see Sarah the next day. After Sarah received a battery of tests and went through days of examinations, Dr. Cerqueira sat quietly in his office. He held back tears as he read Sarah's paperwork. Sarah's test results revealed she had leukemia.

On his way home, Dr. Cerqueira stopped to personally give Sarah's parents the sad news. The leukemia was attacking her small body. Her diagnosis was hopeless. As Dr. Cerqueira sat with Sarah's parents at their kitchen table, he tried to explain that nothing could be done to save her life. Dr. Cerqueira later said, "I don't think I have ever had a more difficult conversation than the one that night."

After a couple of months, Sarah became confined to her bed. She lost her smile, and she lost most of her weight. Dr. Cerqueira, Anna, the pastor, and many, many people from their church stopped by and visited Sarah.

Then one Friday afternoon, Dr. Cerqueira received another telephone call. It was Sarah's mother. She asked him to come and check on Sarah. Dr. Cerqueira hurried to the house. When he arrived, he found Sarah was a small bundle that barely moved. After a short examination, Dr. Cerqueira knew Sarah would soon leave this world. He urged her parents to spend as much time with her as possible.

The next Sunday morning, the church service started as usual. The singing, the sermon all seemed meaningless to Dr. Cerqueira when he thought of Sarah. He felt enveloped in sadness.

At the end of the message, the pastor suddenly stopped speaking. His eyes were wide as he stared at the back of the church. Everyone turned to see what he saw. It was Sarah. Her parents brought her to church for one last visit. She was covered in a blanket, and she held a dandelion in one little hand.

Sarah didn't sit in the back row. Instead, she used all her strength and walked to the front of the church where her vase was still by the pulpit. She placed her flower in the vase and laid a piece of paper beside it. Then she slowly walked back to her parents.

Seeing little Sarah place her flower in the vase for the last time moved everyone. At the end of the service, people gathered around Sarah and her parents, trying to offer as much love, prayer, and support as possible.

> **Did You Know?**
>
> Zephaniah was the great-great-grandson of King Hezekiah. So, he was a person of high social ranking. He was probably a distant relative of King Josiah. The high point in the reign of Josiah was the recovery of the Law by Hilkiah in 622 B.C. (2 Kings 22–23; 2 Chronicles 34). The discovery of the Law caused a revival of Israel spiritually. Baal worship was cut off (Zephaniah 1:4), but otherwise, Judah's moral condition justified the severe judgments that Zephaniah prophesied.

Four days later, Sarah died.

Dr. Cerqueira and Anna sat in the church for Sarah's funeral. The pastor walked up and asked to see them after the funeral. The funeral ended and everyone went to the cemetery. After the graveside service, Dr. Cerqueira and Anna stood at the cemetery near their car as people walked past them. The pastor walked up and in a quiet voice he whispered, "Dave, I've got something you and Anna ought to see." He pulled out of his pocket the piece of paper Sarah left by the vase. He handed the paper to Dr. Cerqueira and said, "You'd better keep this; it may help you in your line of work."

Dr. Cerqueira opened the folded paper to read what Sarah had written. In pink crayon, Sarah wrote:

Dear God,
> *This vase has been the biggest honor of my life.*
>> *–Sarah*

Sarah's note and her vase should help you realize that life is an opportunity to serve God by serving people, and, as Sarah put it, that is the biggest honor of all.

Don't hide from God. Seek the Heavenly Father. Seek holiness. Seek humility. In Jesus' name.

A Moment of Prophecy

Gather yourselves together, yea, gather together, O nation not desired;
Before the decree bring forth, before the day pass as the chaff, before
the fierce anger of the Lord come upon you, before the day of the Lord's
anger come upon you.

– Zephaniah 2:1-2

In this passage, Zephaniah uses a rare verb that derives from gathering chaff or stubble, meaning to "gather what is small and insignificant." He repeats the word twice for emphasis. Having spelled out the judgment up to this point, Zephaniah now begins to call for repentance. He describes what will take place once they are gathered as "the Decree ... the day ... the fierce anger of the Lord" and "the day of the Lord's anger." These are all references to Israel's regathering in the land before the seven-year Tribulation begins. The current nation of Israel is back in its land, in unbelief, but they are positioned to fulfill what the prophets have predicted will happen during the Tribulation.

CHAPTER 10

The Do-Nothing Club

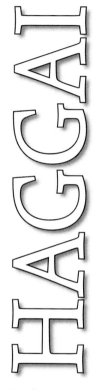

Thus speaketh the Lord of hosts, saying, This people say, The time is not come, the time that the Lord's house should be built.

—Haggai 1:2

Larry Walters was a truck driver. However, his lifelong dream was to fly. When Larry graduated from high school, he joined the Air Force hoping to become a pilot, but his poor eyesight disqualified him. When he left the service, he spent most days sitting in his lawn chair in his backyard. Since he lived near an airport, he sat in his lawn chair, watched planes, and dreamed about flying.

Then one day, Larry Walters got an idea. He went to the Army Surplus Store, and he bought a tank of helium and forty-five heavy-duty weather balloons. He went home and strapped the balloons to his lawn chair. He anchored the chair to the bumper of his Jeep and inflated the balloons with helium. Then he packed some sandwiches and drinks, and a loaded a BB gun. He figured he would shoot out a few of those balloons when it was time to return to Earth.

Larry sat in his chair and on July 2, 1982, he cut the anchoring cord. He thought that he would slowly float up for a short flight. However, things didn't work out that way. When Larry cut the cord, he shot up as if he was fired out of a cannon. He didn't go up a couple of hundred feet. He shot up and leveled off at eleven thousand feet. At that height, he

Haggai

Means "festive" in Hebrew, from the root חָגַג (chagag).

couldn't deflate the balloons or he would unbalance the load and fall. So, he stayed up there. He just floated around for fourteen hours. He was totally at a loss as to how to get down.

Eventually, Larry drifted into the approach corridor for the Los Angeles International Airport. A PAN AM pilot radioed the tower about passing a man in a lawn chair at eleven thousand feet and the man had a gun in his lap. After being up there for fourteen hours, Larry was rescued when a helicopter hovered over him and dropped a rescue line. They used that line to tow him back to Earth.

As soon as Larry hit the ground, he was arrested. As he was being led away in handcuffs, a TV reporter yelled out, "Mr. Walters, why did you do it?" Larry Walters stopped, turned, looked at the reporter, and said, "A man can't just sit around and do nothing."

Larry Walters was right. A man shouldn't sit around and do nothing. However, today, that is what people do. A recent study by the health and lifestyle group, Get America Fit, showed that seventy-eight percent of Americans don't meet the daily requirements for physical activity. Instead, most people spend most of their time sitting. Some sit and watch television. Others sit and play with smartphones. However, most just sit and do nothing.

Sitting and doing nothing is not a recent problem. It has been happening for thousands of years. In 520 B.C., the prophet Haggai addressed a group who wanted to sit around and do nothing.

The Book of Haggai was the first of the three Minor Prophets written after the exile. Haggai is what Bible scholars call a post-exilic prophet. He preached to the remnant, the small group, who came back from exile to rebuild the city of Jerusalem. Some of the prophets preached to the people and told them that their sins would lead them into exile. Some of the prophets preached to the people while they were in exile. However, Haggai lived in a time when the people had returned. The people of God were in exile for seventy years, but now they had returned home. A small group came home to Jerusalem

with a mission from God. They were to rebuild the walls, the city, the temple, and they were to rebuild their relationship with God.

At the beginning of the Book of Haggai, sixteen years had gone by since the remnant returned. Sixteen years had passed, and the walls were still a wreck, the city was in shambles, and the temple was still in ruins. Sixteen years have gone by, and the people did nothing.

The people Haggai preached to were different than the congregation of Amos, Hosea, or Joel. They were not idol worshipers. God broke them of their idolatry.

One of our dogs had a problem with doing his business on the floor. For some reason, this puppy had a difficult time being house trained. So, I called a dog trainer and asked for some advice. Do you know how to get a dog to stop doing his business on your nice shag carpet? You rub his nose in it.

Now, please don't write me nasty letters and emails. I'm just passing on what the dog trainer told me. I'm not promoting being cruel to Fido. I'm just telling you that if you rub a dog's nose where he goes potty, that dog will be happy to go outside to do his business.

For seventy years, the Israelites got their noses rubbed in their own mess. For seventy years, they were in Babylon which was full of idol worshipers. When they came back from Babylon, never again do the children of Israel practice idolatry. God broke them from their idol worship.

So, they were the right people. They were God's people. They came back to the right place to do the right thing, but they did nothing. The people in Haggai's time were members of what I like to call the Do-Nothing Club. They loved the Lord, but they did nothing to contribute to His cause.

Lame Excuses

God sent Haggai with a message for the Do-Nothing Club, and it is a message that is still applicable today. First, Haggai spoke of lame excuses. You see, not only did the people not rebuild God's house, but they also had lame excuses. Notice what Haggai tells them, "Thus speaketh the LORD of hosts, saying, This people say, The time is not come, the time that the LORD's house should be built" (Haggai 1:2).

Timing
The Children of Israel had the lame excuse of timing. They said, "the time is not come" to rebuild the temple. In other words, they said, "The time is not right."

Timing is still a popular excuse today. I have heard people say, "I don't think the timing is right to grow this church." "We shouldn't start any new Sunday school classes; the timing is not right." "We shouldn't reach out to this community; the timing is not right." People have said to me, "I can't join this church; the timing is not right." "I can't get baptized now; the timing is not right." "I can't live for the Lord; the timing is not right."

Over my years in the ministry, I have repeatedly heard the excuse of timing. If you'll pardon me for saying so; Momma always used to say, "Excuses are like backsides. Everyone has a different one and they all stink!"

For sixteen years the people in Haggai's time refused to rebuild the temple because they said the timing was not right. Well, good grief! when is the timing going to be right? If we listen to people like that, we will never do anything for God. Are we going to do something for God? Or are we going to do nothing?

The excuse that breaks my heart the most is when people put off getting saved because the timing is not right. They say, "I'll get around to it. I'm going to get saved someday!" Well, yesterday is gone, and there is no promise of tomorrow. So, if you're going to get saved, you better get saved while you've still got the breath of today.

There is an old legend that tells of a meeting of all of Satan's demons. The devil wanted to figure out how to catch more souls. One demon stood up and said, "I will go to Earth and tell people the Bible is a fairy tale." Another demon said, "I will tell them there is no God, no Savior, no Hell, no Heaven."

Then Satan, the devil himself, stood up and said, "You won't be able to make all of them believe those things. So, we will go to Earth and tell them there is no hurry, to wait for a better time to accept Christ and live for him." That was the plan they came up with, and it has been working until this very day.

Someone may read this book and be almost persuaded to take a stand for Christ, but you put off your decision and say, "Not today, but tomorrow. The timing is not right." I want you to understand the Bible says there is but a step between you and death. Just a step! Anyone could die at any moment. The Bible says life is like a vapor. It is like a puff of smoke. It is here—then it is gone. You just never know when it will be your time. So, if you have not accepted Christ as Savior and Lord, I wouldn't put it off. If you need to rededicate your life to the Lord, I wouldn't put it off. Do it today.

> ### Did You Know?
>
> **Haggai is the second shortest book in the Old Testament.**

Time

Not only did the Jewish people have the lame excuse of timing, but they also had the lame excuse of time. They just didn't have the time. Notice what Haggai says to them: He says, "Is it time for you, O ye, to dwell in your cieled houses, and this house lie waste?" (Haggai 1:4). You see, they didn't have enough time to build God's house, but they had time to build themselves a house.

The word "ceiled" means "paneled." The Jews lived in paneled houses—specifically wood-paneled houses. Why would God make that observation? The answer is found in the book of Ezra, where the people who went back to Jerusalem to rebuild the temple are described. "They also gave money to the masons and the carpenters, and food, drink, and oil to the people of Sidon and Tyre to bring cedar logs from Lebanon to the sea, to Joppa, according to the permission which they had from Cyrus king of Persia" (Ezra 3:7).

What happened to the cedar logs? Where is the wood? Where is the wood they purchased to build the temple? When God's people returned to Jerusalem, instead of using the wood to build the temple, they used the wood to panel their own houses.

You say, "Wow! That's a shame!" Well, is it any different when you know the Bible says that you should give to the Lord, but you take what God gives you and spend it on your house, or on your car, or on your boat? Now there is nothing wrong with hav-

> ### Did You Know?
>
> The actual return to the promised land took place in three main stages. The first group was in 536 when Haggai and Zechariah returned with approximately fifty thousand under the command of Zerubbabel (Ezra 2). It can be reasonably assumed that Haggai was a child upon his return. The second group was not until 457, some seventy-nine years later, led by Ezra. This was around 2,058 people (Ezra 8–10). The third and final group was 445 b.c. and led by Nehemiah, who oversaw the rebuilding of Jerusalem's walls.

ing a house, or a car, or a boat, or things. However, when you take what belongs to God so that you can have those things, it is wrong. God should come first.

Lost Priorities

Haggai speaks of lame excuses and lost priorities. He says, "Now therefore thus saith the LORD of hosts; Consider your ways" (Haggai 1:5). He repeats himself when he says, "Thus saith the LORD of hosts; Consider your ways" (Haggai 1:7). "Consider your ways" means "think about what you are doing." In other words, give thoughtful attention to your ways.

How would you respond today if God asked you to consider your ways? Are your priorities straight? Is God first in your life? Could it be that the problems and frustrations in your life are due to your priorities being wrong?

The people in Haggai's time had problems because of the lost priorities. What kind of problems? Haggai tells them, "Ye have sown much, and bring in little; ye eat, but ye have not enough; ye drink, but ye are not filled with drink; ye clothe you, but there is none warm; and he that earneth wages earneth wages to put it into a bag with holes."

They ate, but they did not get full. They drank, but they were still thirsty. They had clothing, but they were not warm. They had money, but they had nothing to show for it. Why? It was because their priorities were all wrong.

For the most part, I believe Americans have their priorities wrong. We have allowed ourselves to get sidetracked by the cares of this world. The children of Judah were not

> ## Did You Know?
>
> **Seven closely linked Old Testament books describe the post-exilic circumstances of God's covenant people. Three historical books (Ezra, Nehemiah, and Esther) and four prophetic books (Daniel, Haggai, Zechariah, and Malachi) combine to provide a composite picture of the deplorable spiritual and social conditions of the Jewish nation at that time. Yet, despite these impediments, God was able to revive His people through a handful of faithful Jews who had not lost hope in Him.**

doing something bad in and of itself. They were building their houses. The last time I checked, it is not a sin to provide a place to live for your family. What was a sin was that they had their priorities wrong. You may have something in your life right now that you know is not prioritized correctly. You know it has gotten in the way of your spiritual life or your church life, but you may be thinking, "I don't see what is wrong with watching the football game," or "I don't see what's wrong with watching TV," or "I don't see why doing such and such is a problem." And you are right, there is nothing wrong with watching the football game or watching some television, but it becomes a problem when it gets in the way of our relationship with the Lord.

There is an old song that I love called *I'd Rather Have Jesus*. The lyrics go like this, "I'd rather have Jesus than silver or gold, I'd rather be his than have riches untold, I'd rather have Jesus than houses or lands, I'd rather be led by his nail-pierced hands, than to be a king of a vast domain and be held in sin's dread sway. I'd rather have Jesus than ANYTHING this world affords today." I don't know about you, but I would rather have Jesus than anything else.

How about you? Is God your number one priority?

One of the most extraordinary birthday parties ever held occurred a couple of years ago. This birthday party wasn't in a plush ballroom of a grand hotel. There were no famous celebrities at this birthday party. There wasn't anyone rich or powerful at this birthday party. This birthday party was held at three in the morning in a small all-night cafe in Honolulu, Hawaii. The birthday party was held for a prostitute. Most of the guests at the birthday party were prostitutes. And the man who threw the birthday party was a Christian. In fact, he was a pastor named Tony.

The idea to throw this birthday party came to Tony very early one morning as he sat in the cafe. He was drinking coffee at the counter when a group of prostitutes walked in and sat in the stools around him. One of the girls was named Agnes. She was upset because not only was it her birthday tomorrow but that she'd never had a birthday party.

So, Tony thought it would be a great idea to surprise Agnes with a birthday party. He learned from the cafe owner, a man named Harry, that the girls came in every morning around 3:30 a.m. Tony asked Harry if they could use the café for the party. Harry agreed. So, they decorated the café for a party. Word somehow got out on the street, and by 3:15 the next morning, the place was packed with prostitutes, the cafe owner and his wife, and Tony.

When Agnes walked in, she saw streamers, balloons, Harry holding a birthday cake, and everyone screaming out "Happy Birthday!" Agnes was overwhelmed. Tears poured down her face as the crowd sang *Happy Birthday*. When Harry called on her to cut the cake she paused. In her entire life, she had never had a birthday cake. So, she asked if she could take it home to show her mother. When Agnes' party was over, everyone was quiet. Tony did what a Christian should. He led Harry, Harry's wife, and a roomful of prostitutes in a prayer for Agnes.

> ### Did You Know?
>
> In 538, the Persian king, Cyrus, issued a decree allowing the Jews to return to their homeland. Over one hundred and fifty years before this event, Isaiah had prophesied that God would use Cyrus to bring about this restoration (Isaiah 44:24–45:7).

That was a birthday party rarely seen in Honolulu—thrown by a Baptist preacher for a thirty-nine-year-old prostitute who had never had anyone go out of their way to do something like this and who expected nothing in return. Harry, the cafe owner, found it hard to believe some churches would do this sort of thing, but if there were, then that's the sort of church he'd be prepared to join. So, Harry, Harry's wife, Agnes, and several of the prostitutes that were in the café that night, gave their lives to the Lord. They were gloriously and miraculously saved. Lives were changed for all eternity because one man threw a birthday party for a prostitute.

What about you? What will you do for God? Will you get rid of all those lame excuses? Will you get your priorities in the right order? Will you make God the top priority in your life?

Do you want to do something for the Lord? Or are you a member of the Do-Nothing Club?

A Moment of Prophecy

The glory of this latter house shall be greater than of the former, saith the LORD of hosts: and in this place will I give peace, saith the LORD of hosts.

—Haggai 2:9

This prophecy—comparing Solomon's Temple to a future temple—goes beyond the second temple under construction at the time. Some see this prophecy as being fulfilled when Herod expanded the temple. However, only the Millennial Temple (see Ezekiel 40–47) will fulfill this far-reaching prophecy.

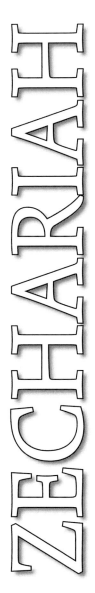

ZECHARIAH

CHAPTER 11

Moving Your Mountains

Who art thou, O great mountain? before Zerubbabel thou shalt become a plain: and he shall bring forth the headstone thereof with shoutings, crying, Grace, grace unto it.

—Zechariah 4:7

J. B. Betts and his wife Marion were the parents of five healthy children when they found themselves facing a mountain. Marion was expecting their sixth child, but her doctor was concerned about the pregnancy. Test results revealed a high probability the baby would be born with Down's Syndrome. Some physicians felt the best option was to terminate the pregnancy.

The Betts family had a deep and strong Christian faith. J. B. was in the music ministry. He and his family traveled all over the United States sharing the gospel in song. Times were tough, but they lived by faith, and God had always been faithful. Still, it would be a struggle taking care of a child with special needs on the road. So, J. B. and Marion stood facing a mountain that seemed impossible to move.

Are you facing mountains in your life? All of us have trials, problems, and heartaches. Sometimes those troubles seem hopeless. However, with God, you can conquer your mountain, but if you are not careful, your mountain will conquer you.

In the time of Zechariah, the people of God faced mountains both figuratively and literally. There was a mountain they had to conquer. So, God sent Zechariah, a man with mountain-moving faith.

Zechariah is another of the post-exilic prophets. He preached to the remnant, the

> ## Zechariah
>
> **From the Hebrew name זְכַרְיָה (Zekharyah) meaning "YAHWEH remembers."**

small group, who came back from exile to rebuild the city of Jerusalem. Some of the prophets preached to the people and told them that their sins would lead them into exile. Some of the prophets preached to the people while they were in exile. But Zechariah lived in a time when the people had returned. After seventy years in exile in Babylon, a small group of people had returned to Jerusalem to rebuild the temple.

When the people came back to rebuild the temple, they had high hopes. However, after they started the work, they felt overwhelmed. They cleared out the rubble and debris that was left from the destruction of the temple and piled it off to the side forming a mountain of trash. The mountain soon became a stumbling block.

The king in Jerusalem at this time was a man named Zerubbabel, and the mountain of debris depressed him. He went out every day and stared at the great mountain. He thought, "There is no way that we will ever get this mess cleaned up. There is no way that we will ever get this mountain cleared." Zerubbabel became depressed and convinced himself the mountain was too much for them. So, work on the temple stopped.

Just when there seemed to be no hope, God sent a messenger of encouragement. He sent the prophet Zechariah. Zechariah's name means, "The Lord remembers." Even his name was a message of encouragement because the people needed to know God had not forgotten them.

A Church Facing Mountains

And said unto me, What seest thou? And I said, I have looked, and behold a candlestick all of gold, with a bowl upon the top of it, and his seven lamps thereon, and seven pipes to the seven lamps, which are upon the top thereof. And two olive trees by it, one upon the right side of the bowl, and the other upon the left side thereof.

—Zechariah 4:2-3

The fourth chapter of Zechariah opens with the prophet being awakened from a deep sleep by an angel. The angel showed Zechariah a vision or a golden candlestick, also known as a lampstand or a menorah. There was a bowl with seven pipes on top of the menorah. On either side, there was an olive tree.

The menorah spoke of the people of the Lord. Even today, one of the symbols of the nation of Israel is the menorah. In the book of Revelation, the Apostle John received a vision of seven menorahs which represented seven churches. So, God's people are the menorah, the candlestick, the lampstand. Jesus said of his followers, "You are the light of the world" (Matthew 5:14). The church faces

mountains today that we must overcome to be the light of the world.

Wrong Attitudes

The church faces the mountain of wrong attitudes.

Many people have the wrong attitude about Jesus. There are more cults in the world today than there have ever been. Statistics show that false religions and cults have deceived multitudes of people.

Islam is growing at an unprecedented rate. There are over 1.3 billion Muslims, of which between 130 million and 260 million are radical extremists. Over sixty-five nations in the world are Islamic, with the population rising in many countries such as the United Kingdom and France.

Millions are being deceived by other world religions. Hinduism has 851 million followers; Buddhism, 375 million; Sikhism, 25 million; Confucianism, 6.4 million; Jainism, 4.5 million; and Shintoism has 2.8 million followers. All these world religions teach a different Jesus than the Jesus of the Holy Bible.

Cults, which used to be on the outside fringes of our society, have grown in popularity and membership. The Church of Jesus Christ of Latter-Day Saints has over 16.5 million members worldwide with over sixty thousand missionaries in one hundred and sixty-five countries. Mormonism is exploding with almost a quarter-million new members being added annually.

Another fast-growing cult is Jehovah's Witnesses. Today, there are over 8 million Jehovah's Witnesses, and over three-quarters of a million of them regularly give fifty hours or more each week to spread their false doctrines door-to-door. It is estimated that more than 5 million so-called "Bible" studies are conducted by Jehovah's Witnesses each month with prospective converts. About two-thirds of current adult Jehovah's Witnesses are converts who were raised in another faith.

Beliefs the majority of Americans held fifty years ago are held by a minority today. Many people today believe there is no Heaven nor Hell, that Jesus is not the virgin-born Son of God, and the Bible is just a book. Church attendance is dropping, with most young people obtaining much of their spiritual input from social media and the Internet.

Many believe the church is not important. I received great criticism in the spring of 2020 during the COVID-19 panic for trying to keep my church open. We practiced social distancing by having drive-in church where people stayed inside their cars in the church parking lot and listened to the service on their car radios. Many people in our community called the police on me for having drive-in church. I had to deal with a government official who said to me, "Church is nonessential."

Wicked Adversary

Not only does the church face the mountain of wrong attitudes, but we also face the mountain of a wicked adversary. We face the devil, Satan, who hates the Lord Jesus Christ and His church. The devil wants to divide us and confuse our minds. The devil doesn't want us to be a light to this dark world.

Many years ago, a young man was invited to a masquerade party. He decided to go, and to dress up like the devil. He went to a costume shop, and he rented a devil costume. It was bright red, with horns and a pointed tail. The costume even came with a red pitchfork.

The costume party wasn't far from where he lived, so he decided to walk. He thought it would be fun for everyone to see him walk through town in his devil costume. As he walked along, a terrible storm blew into town. Suddenly, it started to rain. He thought, *I don't want to mess up this costume.* So, he ran into the first building that he could find that was open. The building he ran into just happened to be a church. The church was packed with people for the Wednesday night prayer meeting.

The congregation was startled when the door burst open and in walked the devil. Just as the people in the church looked up, there was a loud clap of thunder, and the devil came walking down the aisle.

Everyone in the church stopped rejoicing and they started running. They stopped singing and they started screaming. Everybody ran out into the rain except for one elderly woman with a walker. She had to use a walker because she had a bad leg, and she moved very slowly. Now, suddenly, she was face to face with who she thought was the devil himself.

Did You Know?

Zechariah was a contemporary of Haggai. Zechariah delivered his first message about two months after Haggai preached his first message in August of 520 B.C.

The elderly woman looked at the devil and she said, "Oh, Mr. Devil, please don't hurt me." She said, "You need to know that I've gone to this church for thirty years. I'm a Sunday school teacher and I'm a choir member. I've gone to this church for thirty years." She said, "But please don't hurt me. I've been on your side the whole time!"

The point is, the devil tore up that church, and he is still tearing up churches today. The devil is in the business of trashing churches. Satan has declared war on the church. Never have I seen a day when so many churches are being plundered by the devil as they are today. Statistics tell us that eight thousand churches in America each year will just fold up and close their doors and quit. It is estimated that in the United States, seventeen hundred pastors leave the ministry each month, never to return. Only three out of forty pastors make it to retirement. The other thirty-seven quit the ministry for good. The devil is attacking churches all over America and those churches are declining, dying, or decaying.

My Uncle Elmer used to say that he wasn't afraid of the devil because he was married to the devil's sister. Everybody thought that was funny, except for my aunt. However, the devil is not a laughing matter. Satan hates the church, and he is working overtime today to destroy the church.

A Christian Facing Mountains

Then he answered and spake unto me, saying, This is the word of the LORD unto Zerubbabel ...

—Zechariah 4:6a

Not only does the church face mountains, but also Christians face mountains. Zerubbabel was a believer in the One True God, but he faced a personal mountain. Today, if you are a believer in the One True God through His Son, the Lord Jesus Christ, you will also face personal mountains. You will face mountains in your own life.

Right now, some of you face an economic mountain. You have a mountain of bills and debts. It's crushing you. So, you stand and look at that mountain, you say, "There's no hope."

Some of you face the mountain of the unknown. Maybe you're getting ready to leave on a journey. Maybe you're leaving your home, your family, and your friends. Perhaps you're scared.

Some of you face the mountain of the loss of a dream. Life has beaten the hope right out of you. You just walk through the day in a constant state of depression.

Some of you face the mountain of a domestic tragedy. You just can't seem to patch up the mess that your marriage has become. It seems like divorce is the only option you have left.

Some of you face the mountain of loneliness. Every time you reach your hand over to the other side of that empty bed, your heart breaks. You feel like there is nobody in this world who loves you.

Some of you face the mountain of a child that has lost his way. No matter how hard you try, you can't seem to reach that kid. No matter how much you want to, you just can't seem to help that child you love so much.

Some of you face the mountain of personal loss. You have recently had a loved one go on into eternity too soon. Now you are living under the

> ### Did You Know?
>
> **Zechariah was murdered by his own people in the temple court-yard between the temple and the altar. Jesus scolded the Pharisees for their unbelief and likened them to the people who killed Zechariah (see Matthew 23:35).**

cloud of a broken heart. The hurt you feel, the grief you carry, is so big, it's so heavy, that as you stand looking in the face of your grief you say, "I'll never see that mountain move."

Some of you face the mountain of sickness. You've been to one doctor after another, but they just can't seem to help. You just feel terrible all the time.

Is there any hope? Will you ever overcome your mountain?

A Comforter Flattening Mountains

Then he answered and spake unto me, saying, This is the word of the LORD unto Zerubbabel, saying, Not by might, nor by power, but by my spirit, saith the LORD of hosts."

—Zechariah 4:6

Your might, your power, won't overcome your mountains. There is no human power strong enough to overcome the mountains in our lives. However, the Comforter, the Holy Spirit, can flatten your mountain.

In Zechariah's vision, there was a bowl filled with olive oil on top of the menorah. In the time of Zechariah, olive oil was used as fuel for lamps. It is olive oil flowing into the menorah that gives it light. Olive oil is a picture of the Holy Spirit. And it's the Holy Spirit that flows into the church that makes us the light of the world. It is the power of the Holy Spirit that flows into us that gives us the strength to flatten our mountains. Not by might, church. Not by power, church. But by my Spirit says the Lord of hosts.

How do you respond to that mountain? Well, you could ignore it. You could say, "I'm just going to ignore my mountain and play like it's not there." But the mountain is not going to go away. Ignoring it is not the right response.

You could find the easy way around it. You know, numb your mind with drugs, or alcohol, or pleasures of this world. But the easy way is the wrong way. The easy way is the road to disaster. The easy way is the road to death.

Or you could decide to face your mountain. You could decide to defy it. You could stand and look at that mountain and say, "Alright mountain, it's just you and me. But I've got the Lord with

---

Did You Know?

Olive oil is a picture of the Holy Spirit. Consider that oil is a lubricant—there is little friction and wear among those who are lubricated by the Spirit of God. Oil heals and was used as a medicinal treatment in biblical times (Luke 10:34)—the Holy Spirit brings healing and restoration. Oil lights when it is burned in a lamp—the Spirit of God provides light to a dark world. Oil warms when it is used as fuel for a flame—the Spirit of God brings warmth and comfort when He takes up residence in you. Oil invigorates when used to massage—the Holy Spirit invigorates us for His service. Oil adorns when applied as a perfume—the Holy Spirit adorns us and makes us more pleasant to be around. Oil polishes—the Holy Spirit wipes away our grime and smooths out our rough edges.

me. You've met your match. I'm not backing up. I'm not going around you. I'm not giving up. And I'm not surrendering."

How do you respond to your mountain? Well, you realize you're not unique. Everybody has a mountain. You're not the only one with problems. Jesus never said the Christian life would be easy.

John the Baptist got his head cut off. Stephen was stoned to death. Paul was thrown in jail. Shadrach, Meshach, and Abednego were pitched in a fire. Daniel was thrown to the lions. All the disciples of Jesus were killed for their faith. Only John lived to be an old man, but he was sent to prison on the island of Patmos. Who said it was going to be easy? There is no Christian life without mountains.

However, I want you to know your mountain may be the reason you are here. Your mountain may be your purpose. The problem that you are facing may find that you are the solution. You may be like Esther. God placed Esther, a Jew, right into the household of the king of Persia. God made Esther the queen of Persia. And when the plot was discovered to murder all the Jews in the kingdom, Esther discovered her mountain. Her purpose was to save the Jews. God created her for such a time as this.

So, you look at that mountain and you realize God has allowed that mountain to come into your life because that is the mountain you are going to move. This is

> ## Did You Know?
>
> Zechariah contains some of the greatest Old Testament visions of the coming Messiah. Consequently, the New Testament writers either quote directly or allude to fifty-four passages from Zechariah in about sixty-seven different places in the New Testament. The verses most directly quoted are Zechariah 8:16 (Ephesians 4:25), Zechariah 9:9 (Matthew 21:5; John 12:15), Zechariah 11:12–13 (Matthew 27:9–10), Zechariah 12:10 (John 19:37), and Zechariah 13:7 (Matthew 26:31; Mark 14:27).

the mountain you are going to tear down. How? Realize you are not alone. Understand you are not the only one with a mountain. Recognize this may be your finest hour. Then have faith. Faith can move mountains.

I started this chapter by telling you about a mountain J. B. and Marion Betts faced. Remember, J. B. and his wife, Marion, had five children that traveled with them all over the country. The Betts were in the music ministry, and they traveled from church to church performing for the Lord.

When Marion became pregnant with their sixth child, tests revealed a high probability that the baby had Down's Syndrome. Medical professionals suggested that Marion have an abortion, but to the Betts family, that was not an option. J. B. and Marion's sixth child was a boy born with Down's Syndrome. They named him James. For years, James traveled with the family. He wasn't a performer or a musician, but he stood up on stage with his family as they sang.

After many years, J. B. retired from being on the road and moved to Heber Springs, Arkansas. He was hired to be the minister of music at Sugar Loaf Baptist Church in Heber Springs.

J. B. and Marion's youngest son, James—the child who was born with Down's Syndrome—grew up. For the last several years, James has gone around Heber Springs giving out a piece of paper. James works at Walmart. Every day as he greets people, he hands them a piece of paper. If you ask James what he is doing he says, "I am giving out my testimony."

James' testimony touched me so much, that I have decided to include it in this book. This is what James—the young man with Down's Syndrome—wrote:

I was born on January 31, 1972, in Memphis, Tennessee. A few months later the doctors and nurses confirmed that my parents had a Down's Syndrome baby. At first, my parents agonized over the news. They were told that I would be slow in learning. It was suggested that they put me in an institution. They would have never agreed to that. They prayed that the Lord would make me normal like the other children. But that did not happen.

I am the last of six children with fine Christian parents who set the Christian example for me and taught me how to get into God's Word. We lived in the Memphis area and went to a great church, Leewood Baptist Church. When I was twelve years old on Sunday, I went down the aisle and got on my knees, and prayed. I knew that I was lost, and I wanted the Lord to come into my life. That same day, my pastor friend came to my house, and he went through the plan of salvation with me. He asked me if I would like to receive the Lord into my heart. And I told him that I would. I repeated that sentence prayer that he led me in, and I knew that I was saved.

The next Sunday, I was baptized. I knew that I was lost back then and now I knew that the Lord had saved me. When I went to bed that night, I felt a quiet peace in my heart. God saved me on April 21, 1984.

The Bible says in Romans 6:23, "For the wages of sin is death; but the gift of God is eternal life through Jesus Christ our Lord."

And the Bible also says in my favorite verse, John 3:16, "For God so loved the world, that he gave his only begotten Son, that whosoever believeth in him should not perish, but have everlasting life."

And the Bible says in Romans 10:9, "That if thou shalt confess with thy mouth the Lord Jesus, and shalt believe in thine heart that God hath raised him from the dead, thou shalt be saved."

That's how I received eternal life. Have you ever asked the Lord to save you and give you eternal life like I did? You can do that today. Are you a Christian and have backed away from the Lord? You too can have a fresh start. Is God real to you like He is real to me? You and I both have problems. Our problems may be different, but the best life you can ever have is one that is completely surrendered to God.

James' testimony—the testimony of a young man with Down's Syndrome—is amazing. It is the testimony of a man who faced mountains, and by the power of God Almighty, he moved his mountains.

One day a preacher knelt with a twelve-year-old boy named James who had Down's Syndrome. He told him how to get saved and that little boy turned to Christ. Then the Spirit of God came into his life. Now that little boy is out sharing the Gospel and the little church he is a part of in Heber Springs, Arkansas, is on fire for the Lord. People all over Heber Springs have given their life to Christ because of James' testimony written on a piece of paper. Here is a man who faced tremendous mountains, but he overcame them by the power of Christ. Oh, by the way, the town of Heber Springs recently elected James their mayor.

Mayor James Betts

Jesus said if you've got the faith of a grain of mustard seed, you can toss your mountain aside. Speak to the mountain in faith, and the Bible says the mountain has got to move. Stop trying to run around your mountain. Stop trying to ignore your mountain. Face your mountain with the power of the Holy Spirit. Face your mountain with faith. Attack that mountain. Move that mountain. Crush that mountain.

In Jesus Name!

A Moment of Prophecy

No other prophet except for Isaiah spoke more about the Messiah than Zechariah. The book is predominantly apocalyptic and eschatological and through his prophecies he manages to put a real awareness and eagerness into the hearts of the people with his messages of messianic hope.

- The Angel of the Lord (Zechariah 3:1)
- The Righteous Branch (Zechariah 3:8; 6:12–13)
- The King/Priest (Zechariah 6:13)
- The humble King (Zechariah 9:9–10)
- The cornerstone (Zechariah 10:4)
- The Good Shepherd who is rejected and sold for thirty pieces of silver (Zechariah 11:4–13)
- The pierced one (Zechariah 12:10)
- The cleansing fountain (Zechariah 13:1)
- The smitten Shepherd (Zechariah 13:7)
- The coming Judge and righteous King (Zechariah 14)

CHAPTER 12

Bored Beyond Belief

Ye said also, Behold, what a weariness is it! and ye have snuffed at it, saith the LORD of hosts; and ye brought that which was torn, and the lame, and the sick; thus ye brought an offering: should I accept this of your hand? saith the LORD.

—Malachi 1:13

Several years ago, an elderly man called his grown son a week before Father's Day. At this point in his life, the man's son had moved and he lived several hundred miles away from his parents. He was a successful businessman, and he and his wife were raising a family of their own.

When he answered the phone, his father said, "Son, I hate to ruin your Father's Day Week, but I have to tell you that your mother and I are getting divorced. Forty-five years of misery is enough. All we ever do is fuss and fight. So, since you are gone, there just doesn't seem to be any reason for us to stay together." The son said, "Dad, what are you talking about?" His father replied, "We just can't stand the sight of each other anymore. So, we are getting a divorce." The son was very upset, and he exploded back into the phone, "No! You are not getting a divorce. I will take care of this. Don't do a single thing until I get there. I am going to hang up with you and call the airline. My wife, the kids, and I will be there tomorrow. Until then, don't do a thing!"

The old man hung up his phone. He turned, looked at his wife, and said, "Okay. They are all coming for Father's Day, and they are paying their own way."

The point of the story is: Things are not always as they seem. To the son, it seemed that his parents were getting a divorce, but the situation was very different than it appeared.

Malachi faced a similar problem. He preached to people who appeared to be people in love with the Lord. They went through all the motions. They appeared to be worshiping. They seemed to be strong in their faith, but they were actually bored with God and the things of God.

> ### Malachi
>
> From the Hebrew name מַלְאָכִי (Mal'akhi) meaning "my messenger"

Malachi's name means, "My messenger," and he was the last messenger of God in the Old Testament. He wrote the book that bears his name around 400 B.C. Unlike Haggai and Zechariah who encouraged the people to finish building the temple, Malachi preached to people who had finished building the temple. So, when Malachi preached, he was not concerned about the rebuilding of the temple; instead, he was concerned about what was going on inside of the temple.

But ye have profaned it, in that ye say, The table of the LORD is polluted; and the fruit thereof, even his meat, is contemptible.

—Malachi 1:12

God's people rebuilt the Temple. It was a place of worship and sacrifices. However, Malachi said they polluted the table of the Lord. In other words, the people defiled the altar where the sacrifices were offered to God. The problem

> **Date**
>
> Malachi was written around 400 B.C. Chronologically, it was the last book written in the Old Testament.

was with the attitude of the people. They were bored.

Ye said also, Behold, what a weariness is it! and ye have snuffed at it, saith the LORD of hosts. ...

—Malachi 1:13a

When it came to worship, to spiritual matters, to the things of God, the people said, "It is weariness." In other words, they were bored. They were so bored, they "snuffed at it." The word "snuffed" means "sneered." They sneered at worship. They turned their noses up to Almighty God. They turned their noses up to prayer. They turned their noses up at the preaching of the Word of God. They turned their noses up at their faith because they thought it was boring.

Isn't that where we find ourselves in America today? How else do you explain the fact that less than twenty percent of Americans regularly attend church? By the way, that number drops every year. How else do you explain that eight thousand churches in America each year will fold up and close their doors? How else do you explain the fact that seventeen hundred pastors leave the ministry each month, never to return? It is because we are bored.

It is interesting to note that Malachi is speaking of the condition of the people of God just before the First Coming of the Lord Jesus Christ. The Bible also speaks of how the condition of the people of God will be just before the Second Coming of the Lord Jesus Christ. In Chapter three of the book of Revelation, we find a description of a lukewarm church. Jesus said of the Laodicean church that they were neither cold nor hot, so He will, "spue thee out of my mouth."

Have you ever had lukewarm coffee? It's terrible. It's not hot. It's not cold. It's lukewarm. I believe a lukewarm church is a bored church.

The Curse of Boredom

But cursed be the deceiver, which hath in his flock a male, and voweth, and sacrificeth unto the LORD a corrupt thing: for I am a great King, saith the LORD of hosts, and my name is dreadful among the heathen.

—Malachi 1:14

If you will bear with me, I want to point out a few things about boredom, and I hope I don't bore you. First, I want you to notice that boredom is a curse. Boredom in your spiritual life is a curse. The Bible says that Malachi's congregation was cursed because they deceived themselves with their boredom.

Now let's get real. Have you ever been bored in your spiritual life? If you would just be honest, you would have to say, "I'm bored. Bored with church. Bored with the music. Bored with my Bible. Bored with prayer. I'm bored with the whole church scene. I'm bored! Bored! Bored! Bored!" However, when you have that attitude, your problem is not with the church, the pastor, or God. No, when you have that attitude, your problem is in your heart.

Boredom Will Leave You Cheerless

Boredom will leave you cheerless. When you are bored, you are unhappy. It doesn't seem to me that the people in Malachi's day had much joy. The Bible says they sneered at God. That doesn't seem very joyful to me.

I don't know about you, but I don't like anybody that turns their nose up at anybody. I don't like snooty people. Do you?

> ### *Did You Know?*
>
> **Malachi was the last messenger in the Old Testament. In Malachi 3:1, he reveals that God will send a future messenger to prepare the way for the Messiah. That next messenger was John the Baptist, the first prophet of the New Testament (Matthew 11:10; Mark 1:2–3; Luke 1:76; 7:26–27).**

When I was a little boy, I remember one of our neighbors, Mrs. Seastrunk, won some money playing the lottery. When she got her money, Mrs. Seastrunk changed. She acted snooty. She dropped the names of all her high-class friends. She quit eating at the Crossroads Truck Stop Café, and she took her meals at a fancy uppity restaurant called Sergio's. Mrs. Seastrunk went to charm school. She sipped her coffee with her little pinky finger extended out. She became uppity and acted as if she was better than all of us country bumpkins.

One day after church, Mrs. Seastrunk said to the pastor, "Preacher, you are wearing a three-button suit, and you do not have one button buttoned." She said, "I want you to know that etiquette is that you should button up the top button and the second button but leave open the bottom button. However, you do have the option to only button the center button with a three-button suit."

I don't know about you, but I can't figure all that out. So, I just button up all my buttons. Besides, I'm sure happy that I'm not one of those big-shot TV preachers. I saw a preacher on TV with sixteen buttons. I sure wouldn't know what buttons to button on a sixteen-button suit.

Anyway, we all knew where Mrs. Seastrunk came from. She really didn't impress anyone. She was just like the rest of us. I mean, I was born poor. I was born in the back of a pick-up truck and raised on beans and taters. So, get off all the hooty-flooty stuff.

Mrs. Seastrunk soon found herself without any friends. Even her family avoided her. Even though she had all that money, I don't remember ever seeing her smile.

Like Mrs. Seastrunk, the people in Malachi's time also became uppity. However, instead of turning their nose up at people, they turned their nose up at God.

Boredom Will Leave You Controlled

In addition to leaving you cheerless, boredom will leave you controlled. Boredom will become your master because you try to get out of your state of boredom. You spend your life trying to find something to make you happy. Why else would grown people strap a rubber band around their ankles and jump off a bridge?

When I was in the service, some friends and I had a weekend pass in Southern California. We went to an amusement park called Knox Berry Farm. My friend Dan decided to ride a contraption that looked like a saucer. A machine pulled down the saucer like an old-time slingshot. Dan was pulled back until the cables were tightly stretched. Suddenly, it let go and Dan was thrust way up into the sky.

The next day, Dan told me that ever since he rode the slingshot ride, he had trouble concentrating. I said, "Dan, the reason you can't concentrate is because your bladder is where your brain used to be."

It's a curse when recreation begins to replace the things of God. There is nothing wrong with recreation, but recreation is the side thing. It's not the main thing. The Lord Jesus Christ is the main thing.

Many people become involved with destructive habits because of boredom. Because of boredom, people turn to the bottle or drugs. Because of boredom, some have an affair. Because of boredom, people waste their money gambling. Boredom can cause your life to be controlled by destructive behavior.

Boredom Will Leave You Consumed

Boredom will not only leave you cheerless and controlled, but it will also leave you consumed. Boredom will consume your life.

Master Sergeant Vanhooser was a friend that I served with for many years in the U.S. Army. He worked his entire life thinking about retirement. That was all he used to talk about. He would say, "I can't wait until I retire. Then I will really start living." Master Sergeant Vanhooser lived for his retirement. He worked for his 401(k) savings account and his pension. He worked his whole life so that he would have enough money to live on when he retired. He worked from seven a.m. to five p.m., five or six days a week.

Finally, the day came for Master Sergeant Vanhooser to retire. We had a party, and we gave him a gold watch. Then he went home. All he did was sit in the house and watch TV.

Soon this healthy man, who still had years to live, became ill. He began to have all types of health problems. He never moved. He didn't stay active. He just sat there. All he did was feed his mind with all the depressing stuff that was coming through that TV. One day, he woke up old, feeble, and miserable. Do you know why? He had enough to live on but had nothing to live for.

My friend Master Sergeant Vanhooser just sat on his front porch in one of those Cracker Barrel rocking chairs. From daylight to dusk, he just sat there and let his wife bring his meals. Then he went in the house at five and watched the news where he heard about wars, rapes, murders, child abuse, and the world going to hell. Then he watched "Wheel of Fortune" and a couple of shows that were meaningless. That was his life. Sit on the porch and watch TV. One day his wife walked out on the porch, and he was dead in his Cracker Barrel rocker.

Understand, you may retire from an earthly job, but you never retire from serving the Lord Jesus. You never retire from church, Bible study, prayer, witnessing, and fellowshipping with other believers. You never retire from your relationship with God.

I love the story about the elderly man who sat one day in his yard with his wife. At that point in their lives, they had been married for over sixty years. The wife leaned over and said, "Honey, don't you remember how when we were young, you used to sit close to me?" So, the old man got up and moved next to her. He got close and put his arm around her. She said, "Honey, don't you remember how

Did You Know?

Malachi 4:6 is the last sentence in the Old Testament, and it mentions the word "curse" which is a result of sin. The last sentence in the New Testament (Revelation 22:21) uses the word "grace," the wonderful result of God's love and forgiveness through Jesus Christ.

when you were younger, you always used to kiss me?" So, he puckered up and he planted one right on her. He gave her a romantic kiss. Then she said, "Honey, don't you remember how when you were younger, you used to nibble on my ear?" The old man stood up and started walking toward the house. His wife yelled, "Where are you going?" He turned and said, "To get my teeth!"

The point is you don't retire from a love relationship, and you don't retire from loving the Lord Jesus Christ. Now, it may take you a little longer to get to church, and it may take you a little longer when you get there to remember where you are, but you don't ever retire from church. You don't ever retire from studying your Bible. You don't ever retire from worshiping God. Because there's joy in living for Jesus Christ.

The Cheapness of Boredom

Ye said also, Behold, what a weariness is it! and ye have snuffed at it, saith the LORD of hosts; and ye brought that which was torn, and the lame, and the sick; thus ye brought an offering: should I accept this of your hand? saith the LORD.

—Malachi 1:13

In addition to being cursed, spiritually bored people are cheap. You know, I've never gotten away with trying to be cheap. I bought an aftermarket, cheap radiator hose for my truck. The hose burst the next day. I ended up going back and buying the hose that I should have got in the first place. Anytime, I've tried to get off cheap, it's ended up costing me more.

Do you think that you can be cheap with God? The people in Malachi's time tried. They brought "that which was torn, and the lame, and the sick" as an offering to God. They brought offerings they didn't want. They brought offerings that cost them absolutely nothing. Malachi 1:14 says they made a vow to give God the best ram from their flock. However, instead, they brought God their worthless leftovers.

Today, many people do the same thing. They refuse to give God their best time, effort, or emotions. They give God what is leftover. They give Him what they can do without.

The Jewish people in Malachi's time were spiritually cheap and self-focused. They wanted the best for themselves. That's the reason they didn't give their best male ram. It's because they wanted it. They were selfish.

Have you noticed that we have raised a generation of kids that are so selfish they don't care about anything but themselves? Kids today say, "I want. I want. I want," and we have just lavished things on them.

One day, my wife and I were shopping, and we noticed a little boy with his mom. The child wanted a toy, but his mom said, "No." So, he threw a fit. Then his mom said, "Don't cry. Don't cry. I'll get you that toy. Just don't cry."

I don't know about you, but I was raised differently. If I would have acted like that little boy, my folks would have said, "You want to cry? I'll give you something to cry about! Turn around here." That's what my folks used to say to me, and I don't think they got that from some modern psychology book.

When you give a kid everything they want, they don't respect you. The child becomes bored. It's the same with the spiritual. When we are self-focused and everything is all about us, we are spoiled brats. However, when we get focused on God—when we put God first—then we can let Jesus live through us.

The Cure for Boredom

Spiritually bored people are cursed and cheap, but there is a cure. What is the cure for boredom? Let me suggest a couple of ways.

Serve

First, *serve*. Stop worrying about yourself and start helping somebody else. Pray for people. Give to others. Help someone. Be an encourager.

Several years ago, I went to the hospital to pray for a woman named Ginger

Patterson. Ginger was fighting a losing battle with cancer. So, I went there to pray. I went to the hospital to serve the Lord, but when they wheeled Ginger into the room, God showed up with her. She spoke about God having everything under control. She was so full of Jesus that she glowed. She said, "I've put it in the hands of the Lord." The more she talked, the more I was encouraged. I left the hospital thinking, "I don't know if I was a blessing, but I sure got a blessing.

The best way to get a blessing is to be a blessing to someone else. Serve others and you'll stop being bored.

Seek

Second, *seek*. Seek God. Sadly, most people today do not seek a relationship with God through His Son, Jesus Christ. Instead, they seek ritual religion.

In Malachi 1:14, God says, "I am a great King." We serve a great King. Go out into the world and tell others about that King. You don't bring a great King your leftovers. You give your King your best.

How can you exchange ritual for a relationship with God? Remember that He is a King. Each day, you can come into the presence of a great King. When you pray, you have an audience with the King. When you serve the Lord, you are on a mission from the King.

How can you be bored when you realize that the King became a man? How can you be bored when you look at a blood-stained cross and see Jesus dying in agony? How can you be bored when you see the stone rolled away? How can you be bored when you see a living Jesus coming out of the tomb? The stone was rolled away, and King Jesus is alive! If that doesn't get you excited, then something is wrong with you!

Several years ago, a young Christian man named Will decided to leave Bible college and instead focus on a business career. Will thought he could do more for God in the corporate world. So, he went to college and received his degree in Business Administration. Then he got a job with a Fortune 500 Company.

The years went by, and Will became a young and very successful executive. One day, Will was driving down a suburban street in his brand-new black Jaguar. Suddenly a brick was thrown from the sidewalk, thumping into the side of the car.

Will slammed on the brakes. He ground into reverse. The tires on the Jaguar spun quickly as he zoomed back to the spot from where the brick had been thrown. Will jumped out, grabbed the kid who had thrown the brick, and pushed him up against a parked car. "What was that all about?!" he screamed. "That's my new Jag. That brick you threw is going to cost you a lot of money!"

The young boy said, "Please, mister, please ... I'm sorry! I didn't know what else to do! I threw the brick because no one else would stop!" Tears dripped down the boy's chin as he pointed around the parked car. He said, "It's my brother, mister. He rolled off the curb and fell out of his wheelchair and I can't lift him up." Crying, the boy asked, "Sir, would you please help me get him back into his wheelchair? He's hurt and he's too heavy for me."

Will's anger left him. The mood was transformed in a moment as he realized what had happened. He lifted the young man into the wheelchair and took out his handkerchief and wiped the scrapes and cuts. He then watched as the younger brother pushed him down the sidewalk toward their home.

Will decided to never fix the dented side door of his Jaguar. He kept the dent to remind him not to go through life so fast that someone must throw a brick at him to get his attention.

Maybe you have become so spiritually bored that God has had to throw a brick at you to get your attention? Maybe Malachi's message is the brick that God is throwing at you?

Serve ... Seek ... That's the cure for boredom ... In Jesus Name.

A Moment of Prophecy

In Malachi 4:5, God says that He will send Elijah the prophet. Preceding the First Coming of Jesus was John the Baptist, who came in the "spirit and power" of Elijah (Luke 1:13–17). Had Jesus been accepted by His people, John would have fulfilled the prophecy completely (Matthew 11:13–14). However, since He was rejected, this prophecy awaits a future Elijah (Matthew 17:11–12). John the Baptist did not claim to be Elijah. In fact, he specifically denied it (John 1:21), but he did fill the role of the forerunner for the Messiah's First Coming. Elijah, who appeared with Jesus on the Mount of Transfiguration, will be one of the two witnesses forecast in Revelation 11:1–3 who will prophesy during three and one-half years of the Tribulation in Jerusalem. Orthodox Jews at the Passover set an empty chair for Elijah in every home observance because of Malachi 4:5. Jesus affirmed this prophecy when He said, "Elias truly shall first come and restore all things" (Matthew 17:11).

How To Receive Jesus Christ

1. Admit your need (I am a sinner).
2. Be willing to turn from your sins (repent).
3. Believe that Jesus died for you and rose from the grave
4. Through prayer, invite Jesus Christ to come in and control your life through the Holy Spirit (receive Him as Lord and Savior).

What To Pray

Dear Lord Jesus,

I know that I am a sinner and I need Your forgiveness. I believe that You died for my sins. I want to turn from my sins. I now invite You to come into my heart and life. I want to trust and follow You as Lord and Savior.

In Jesus' Name. Amen.

Bibliography

Briscoe, D. Stuart. *Taking God Seriously: Major Lesson from the Minor Prophets.* Waco, Texas: Word Press, 1986.

Bullock, C. Hassell. *An Introduction to the Old Testament Prophetic Books.* Chicago: Moody Press, 1986.

Cahn, Jonathan. *The Book of Mysteries.* Lake Mary, Florida: Charisma House Book Group, 2016.

Church, J. R. *They Pierced the Veil ... and Saw the Future.* Oklahoma City: Prophecy Publications, 1993.

Claypool, John. *The Preaching Event.* New York: Church Publishing, Inc., 2003.

Durant, Will and Ariel Durant. *The Age of Voltaire.* New York: Simon & Schuster, 1965.

Feinberg, Charles L. *The Minor Prophets.* Chicago: Moody Press, 1990.

Freeman, J. M. and J. H. Chadwick. *Manners & Customs of the Bible.* North Brunswick, New Jersey: Bridge-Logos Publishers, 1998.

Gaebelein, Frank E. *Four Minor Prophets.* Chicago: Moody Press, 1970.

Hubbard, David Allan. *Will We Ever Catch Up with the Bible? The Minor Prophets Speak to Us Today.* Glendale, California: G.L. Publications, 1977.

Hunter, John E. *Major Truths from the Minor Prophets.* Grand Rapids: Zondervan Publishing, 1977.

Ironside, H. A. *Minor Prophets.* Neptune, New Jersey: Bible Truth Depot, 1988.

James, Kyle. "The Town That Sibling Rivalry Built, and Divided." *DW News,* March 7, 2006, page 11–13.

Levy, David M. *Malachi: Messenger of Rebuke and Renewal.* Bellmawr, New Jersey: Friends of Israel, 1992.

McGee, J. Vernon. *Through The Bible Volume IV.* Nashville: Thomas Nelson, 1983.

Morgan, G. Campbell. *The Minor Prophets: The Men and Their Messages.* London: Pickering & Inglis Limited, 1960.

Rhodes, Ron. *End Time Super Trends.* Eugene, Oregon: Harvest House Publishers, 2017.

Shon, Emily. "Why the Great Molasses Flood was So Deadly." History.com, January 15, 2019.

Spargimino, Larry. *Digging Deeper.* Oklahoma City: Beacon Street Publishing, 2021.

The Holy Bible: King James Version.

Walker, James K. *The Concise Guide to Today's Religions and Spirituality.* Eugene, Oregon: Harvest House Publishers.

Wiersbe, Warren W. *The Bible Exposition Commentary Volume 2.* Wheaton, Illinois: Victor Books, 1996.

Williams, Jeff. "Facts About Laziness." GetAmericaFit.org, March 10, 2020.

About The Author

James Collins is the Staff Evangelist for Southwest Radio Ministries. He previously served in various pastoral positions in Kansas, Oklahoma, Illinois, and California. Before being called to SWRC, James was a chaplain in the United States Army and served in Operation Enduring Freedom, Operation Iraqi Freedom, Operation New Dawn, and Operation Inherent Resolve.

A lifelong learner, James has four graduate degrees including a Doctor of Ministry and a Doctor of Theology degrees. He loves reading, especially books on Bible prophecy.

James is married to the love of his life, Amanda Collins. They share their home with their three children, three dogs, and a lifetime collection of books.

If you were blessed by this book, James would love to hear from you. You can reach him by mail at PO Box 76834, Oklahoma City, OK 73147, or by email at info@swrc.com. Also, if you were blessed by this book, James would appreciate if you would leave a review on Amazon and Goodreads.

ALSO AVAILABLE FROM BEACON STREET PRESS

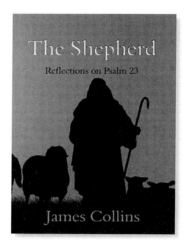

The Shepherd

Reflections on Psalm 23

In *The Shepherd*, James Collins explores the rich meaning behind the world's best known and most loved poem, the Twenty-Third Psalm. The author teaches the psalm verse-by-verse, explaining its extraordinary power to change lives and ease our troubles. He shares its context and colorful background. You will fine encouragement to enjoy the "green pastures' of life while becoming strengthened by the "dark valleys." Through Collins' explanation of the biblical text that illustrates the love and care of the Lord, The Shepherd will help you rediscover the joy, inspiration, and peace of this beloved psalm.

Get your copy today at
www.swrc.com

The real story of Christmas.

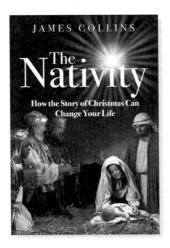

The Nativity

The story of the birth of Jesus Christ as told in Luke 2 is the best-known story in the Bible. To many, the story of God becoming a man—of God taking on human flesh—has become so common that the greatest miracle in history has lost its impact. That's why *The Nativity* was written, to help you take a fresh look at the Christmas story—to help you see beyond the familiar and find the true Spirit of Christmas. Turn the pages to find the answers:

- » Who was the innkeeper?
- » Why is Jesus called Emmanuel?
- » Was Jesus born on December 25?
- » What was the Tower of the Flock?
- » Is Jesus coming back?

Get your copy today at
www.swrc.com